Facts On File Encyclopedia of

IN AMERICA

Science, Health, and Medicine

Encyclopedia of Black Women
in America

Facts On File Encyclopedia of

Black Women

IN AMERICA

Science, Health, and Medicine

Darlene Clark Hine, Editor

Kathleen Thompson, Associate Editor

 Facts On File, Inc.

Facts On File Encyclopedia of Black Women in America: Science, Health, and Medicine

Facts On File, Inc.
11 Penn Plaza
New York, NY 10001

Library of Congress Cataloging-in-Publication Data

Facts on File encyclopedia of Black women in America / Darlene Clark
Hine, editor ; Kathleen Thompson, associate editor.
p. cm.
Includes bibliographical references and index.
Contents: v. 1. The early years, 1619–1899—v. 2. Literature—
v. 3. Dance, sports, and visual arts—v. 4. Business and professions—
v. 5. Music—v. 6. Education—v. 7. Religion and community—
v. 8. Law and government—v. 9. Theatre arts and
entertainment—v. 10. Social activisim—v. 11. Science, health,
and medicine.
ISBN 0-8160-3424-9 (set : alk. paper)
ISBN 0-8160-3428-1 (Science, Health, and Medicine)
1. Afro-American women—Biography—Encyclopedias. I. Hine,
Darlene Clark. II. Thompson, Kathleen.
E185.96.F2 1997
920.72′08996073—dc20   96-33268

Text design by Cathy Rincon
Cover design by Smart Graphics

Printed in the United States of America

RRD VCS 10 9 8 7 6 5 4 3 2 1

This book is printed on acid-free paper.

Contents

How to Use This Volume

SCOPE OF THE VOLUME

The *Science, Health, and Medicine* volume includes entries on individuals and organizations in the following subject areas: midwifery, nursing, medicine, and science.

RELATED OCCUPATIONS

Professionals in related occupations covered in other volumes of this encyclopedia include the following: administrators of health care institutions (*Religion and Community*), aviators (*Business and Professions*), educators (*Education*), and health care advocates (*Religion and Community and Social Activism*).

HOW TO USE THIS VOLUME

The introduction to this volume presents an overview of the history of black women in science, medicine, and health care. A chronology following the bibliographical entries lists important events in the history of black women in these fields in the United States.

Individuals and organizations are presented in alphabetically arranged entries. If you are looking for an individual or organization that does not have an entry in this volume, please check the alphabetically arranged list of the entries for all volumes of this encyclopedia that appears at the end of this book, in addition to the contents of each of the other volumes in this series.

Names of individuals and organizations for which there are entries in this or other volumes of the encyclopedia are printed in **boldface.** Check the contents list at the back of this book to find the volume where a particular entry can be found.

Introduction

On September 12, 1992, a young black woman stepped into the space shuttle *Endeavour*. Soon the shuttle would be launched on a one-week mission to study the effects of zero-gravity on people and animals, but nothing its crew discovered would be of more historical importance than the inclusion of this crew member. **Mae Jemison,** chemist and astronaut, represented the hopes and the achievements of generations of black women who stood outside the scientific establishment. She was a surrogate for women who had yearned to peer into the secrets of life and had been kept away from the microscopes, women who had gazed at the stars in wonder but found the observatories closed to them.

But she also represented all those remarkable women who found a way, however difficult and obscure, to serve the cause of science. A hundred years before, Mae Jemison might have been one of a handful of black women doctors whose determination took them through medical schools where they were scorned and discriminated against. Or she might have been a nurse, struggling for dignity in a Southern hospital. She might have been a science teacher, barred from graduate schools, reading and learning in public libraries, and passing on the thirst for scientific knowledge to black children in underequipped classrooms.

In few areas have black women met more resistance than in science and medicine. They have split more legal hairs in court than they have split atoms in laboratories. They have acted more parts on stage than they have discovered new stars. They have recorded more platinum records than they have discovered new metal alloys. Discrimination against women is as strong in scientific research as it is in the United States Senate. And discrimination against ethnic minorities is subtle but enormously powerful.

Still, black women have made and continue to make their mark in medicine and the sciences. Wherever they could substitute determination and ingenuity for financial and educational resources, they have made successes. And where they could not, they have made dents.

EARLY HEALTH CARE PROVIDERS

Black women, from the time they first stepped onto American shores, have been important providers of health care in this country. The irony of their participation is that, the more formalized the system became, the more they were pushed out of it.

Nursing the sick was, for thousands of years, the job of mothers, sisters, daughters,

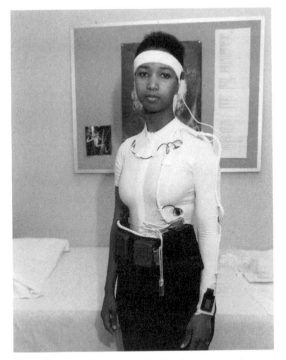

Before she could even think about stepping into the space shuttle Endeavour, *Mae Jemison had to be trained by NASA scientist Patricia Cowings to use biofeedback to control her body's reaction to weightlessness. This photograph shows Jemison dressed in the Cowings-designed apparatus used for the training.* (NASA)

and whatever servants—usually female—a family could afford to hire to help them. Male doctors were called in for serious illnesses, broken bones, and tractor accidents, and the informal nurses followed their orders, for the most part. But for the ordinary medical problems of life, women took care of things. These ordinary problems ranged from colds to influenza to childbirth. They included most injuries that did not threaten life or limb and some that did.

Over the centuries, medical science has stumbled its way toward an understand-ing of the human body and its diseases. In the meantime, women have passed down from generation to generation knowledge about how to treat a croupy cough or what herb to use to draw the poison out of a bee sting.

Black women in early America provided health care in two ways. First, they were usually the only source of care in slave quarters and free black communities. And second, they often took care of white families as slaves or servants. They drew on the knowledge and skills of generations of black women instead of formal education, but, especially in rural areas, the entire population of a neighborhood, black and white, depended on them.

Black midwives were especially crucial in the rural South. One Virginia physician, before the Civil War, estimated that black midwives attended the births of half the white women in the state. A slave midwife was valuable to her white master because of the fees he was able to charge for her services. Some of them, including a woman named Mildred Graves, were known to have made a great deal of money for their owners. One midwife, **Biddy Mason,** traveled across the country from Mississippi to California with her master's family. Promised her freedom at the end of the journey, she had to go to court to get it. Later, she founded a nursery and day-care center in Los Angeles.

The skills that women developed in nursing their families and those who employed them as domestic help were often carried into other areas. During wartime, for example, women went onto the battlefields to nurse soldiers. During the Civil War, many black nurses served the Union army. **Susie Baker King Taylor,** for example, was both laundress and nurse for the first South Carolina Volunteers, a black battalion of which her husband was a member. She wrote about the experience in an autobiography published in 1902.

After the Civil War, African-American midwives and nurses continued to serve their communities. Some freedwomen were even able to earn their living as midwives. Black midwives usually were older women, with children of their own, who believed they had been divinely called to their vocation. Similarly, a black midwife usually recruited her successor in response to a dream or other supernatural instruction. Many midwives also were the daughters and granddaughters of midwives, the call to this special work extending through generations.

Black midwives usually were called "grannies" or "granny midwives," a respectful acknowledgment of age and status, and often they were addressed with a fictive familial name, such as aunt or auntie. Up until the latter part of the twentieth century, the black midwife was a revered member of her community. This continued to be true in spite of modern medicine's revolution in childbirth practices.

All midwives came under vicious attack in the early decades of the twentieth century. At that time, obstetricians were trying to raise the status of their new medical specialty. So, they launched a nationwide campaign blaming midwives for the alarming rates of maternal and infant mortality. Although several contemporary studies proved the competence of lay midwives—the immigrant midwife in the North and the black granny midwife in the South—physicians succeeded in convincing state legislatures that lay midwives should either be prohibited by statute or carefully regulated.

At that time, in the South, physicians were unprepared to take over the midwives' large caseload. Thus, most Southern states accepted the granny midwife as a necessary evil for the time being, and proposed that her alleged abuses be curbed through education, licensing, and supervision. Black midwives continued to deliver babies for substantial numbers of black women in the rural South well into the twentieth century.

For example, in the early 1900s, black midwives may well have delivered most of the babies born in South Carolina. In 1914, black midwives probably attended half of all births in Virginia. In 1936, 67 percent of all North Carolinian black women giving birth were attended by black midwives. As late as 1950, the majority of childbearing black women in Alabama relied on the care of granny midwives. And when today's regional statistics for midwife-attended births are analyzed, midwifery emerges as a primarily rural, Southern, and non-white institution.

Historically, black midwives have been much more prevalent in the southern United States than in other regions because of the region's large African-American population. However, segregation, racism, rural isolation, poverty, and the lack of alternative institutions have all been factors that kept the black midwife in business around the country despite the growing trend toward hospital births.

The quality of the black midwife's services also maintained her popularity among select populations. In addition to attending the childbirth, the midwife usually stayed with the new mother for the early postpartum period, caring for her and the baby and, if necessary, attending to various domestic tasks. Some midwives cultivated relationships with doctors so as to serve their rural communities better. The midwife attended normal deliveries and called on the doctor when complications arose.

Moreover, hospital births, or even physician-attended home births, were economically out of reach for many rural black families through the first half of the twentieth century. In 1924, a black Texas woman reported that she could hire a mid-

Beginning in 1945, Arkansas public health nurse Mamie O. Hale's job was to train black granny midwives how to deliver babies safely. At the time, virtually all the black babies in the state were delivered at home without medical supervision. (UNIVERSITY OF ARKANSAS FOR MEDICAL SCIENCES)

wife for 75 cents while a doctor would charge $15.

The situation of black nurses in this country paralleled that of midwives. Before Florence Nightingale started the modern movement toward formal training for nurses, black women were valued, accepted health care providers. As nursing schools were founded and the profession was licensed, they were pushed further and further out of the field.

NURSING

Before Florence Nightingale, most nurses were not trained professionals having the respect of doctors and patients. They were drudges and scrub ladies with no medical knowledge and, often, little commitment to their work.

That's a harsh judgment, but a true one. Nurses were hired from the least-educated, poorest levels of society, because no one else would do the job. It was ill-paid, dirty, and dangerous, in part because hospitals were appalling places where sick people went to die. Contagious diseases spread through them like wildfire, and sanitation was so poor that infection was a constant threat. The average person viewed hospitals with terror, and rightly so.

During the second half of the nineteenth century, medicine as a profession began to grow up. Medical science was making important discoveries with regard to anesthetics and hygiene. Doctors were able to heal people whom, a decade or two before, they would only have been able to watch die.

Florence Nightingale and her followers were determined that nursing would play an important role in the new medical world. They advocated training for nurses that was almost military in its strictness and thoroughness. Champions of the new nursing were fanatical in their insistence on professionalism, moral uprightness, and respectability, but they knew they had a long way to go from those very sad beginnings.

The history of the development of the nursing profession is a dramatic story of the struggle of a group of women to overcome social, educational and economic adversities. Within this history, however, there runs another, almost parallel, chronicle of the effort of black women to acquire education, to end economic discrimination, and to win professional acceptance from their white counterparts.

During the early phases of the nursing profession in America, a number of concerns riveted the attention of most white leaders in the nursing field. They worried about the exploitation of student nurses in hospital training schools. They were acutely aware that there were limited employment opportunities for graduate nurses, a situation made worse by competition from untrained women. And they were very concerned about the absence of certification or licensing boards and the need to develop collegiate nursing programs. At the same time, they realized that in order to reform nursing and attract women of excellence into the profession, they would have to raise the low social status and esteem accorded to nurses.

The first three American nurse training schools were established in 1873. These early schools operated within hospitals. However, they followed the traditions initiated by Florence Nightingale's move-

ment in Britain in the 1850s to establish an organized system for the training of nurses. As a result, they were characterized by a degree of independence and authority for the faculty, a separate funding apparatus, and the use of women as nurse supervisors.

This was a model situation in many ways, but it didn't last. There wasn't enough money, for one thing. And there was a demand for more science instruction than this sort of school could provide at that time. As a result, the relatively independent nurse training schools were replaced by hospital schools, which came to dominate nursing education.

There were fifteen hospital nurse training schools in 1880 and 431 schools twenty years later. The number of graduates increased from 157 to 3,456 within this time. The growth of nurse training schools continued as hospitals garnered increased respectability from the public, which began to accept them as places of good care, not dens of death. By 1926, there were 2,150 schools with 17,000 graduates. And virtually all of these schools excluded black women.

The hospital nurse training schools were generally very bad. Students were expected to work in the hospital, taking care of patients, often without being paid. Their shifts were long and left little or no time for instruction or study. Students learned only what they picked up on the job. In addition, even trained nurses were not given much respect. They were treated more as servants than as health professionals, both by doctors and by patients. And these were the white nurses!

The situation led nurse leaders to organize what would be renamed, in 1911, the

American Nurses Association (ANA). Its official organ, the *American Journal of Nursing,* had begun publication in 1901. The National League of Nursing Education, the ANA, and many other emerging national societies struggled to upgrade the status of nurses and to professionalize nursing.

You would think that this struggle for better education, working conditions, and status would benefit all nurses. But it didn't. In fact, the professionalization of nursing had a negative impact on black nurses. As training became a necessary qualification for nursing jobs, black nurses were denied the opportunity to get the training. As white women worked to raise the status of the profession, they tried to shut out women who were of lower social status.

In order to understand what black nurses were up against, it is important to understand how the medical establishment worked—and didn't work—for black people at that time. What happened when a black person got sick?

To begin with, many African Americans received no medical treatment at all, especially in rural areas. White doctors did not set up practices in black towns or in the black neighborhoods of larger cities. As for black doctors, by 1890, there were only about 900 of them in the entire country, serving a total black population of seven and a half million.

Sometimes, white hospitals set aside separate wards for the treatment of black patients, but the care in those wards was frequently very bad. In some cases, a black "ward" would consist of a few beds in the basement. Medical treatment was provided by white doctors whose primary concern was for their white patients. Usually, black doctors were not allowed to treat patients in white hospitals, even in these separate wards.

Black nurses had once been tolerated in white hospitals because of the servantlike status of nurses in general. As nursing grew in respectability, however, they were shut out of both hospitals and training schools. The only alternative was to found their own network of nursing schools and hospitals.

In 1886, John D. Rockefeller contributed the funds for the establishment of a school of nursing at the Atlanta Baptist Seminary (now **Spelman College**), a school for black women. This was the first school of nursing established within an academic institution in the country. The earliest black hospital nursing schools came into existence in the 1890s, established mostly by black physicians and black women's clubs, who would play a tremendously important role in black health care.

In 1891, for example, Daniel Hale Williams, a prominent black open-heart surgeon, founded Provident Hospital and Nurse Training School in Chicago. **Fannie Barrier Williams,** a leading Chicago clubwoman, was very active in raising funds for the hospital. She was also involved in the administration of the hospital. While the Provident accepted took both black and white patients, Barrier Williams argued that its training school should be restricted to black nurses because "there are other training schools for white women, but none at all for colored women. Why let white women take any of the few places we'll have open?"

Within a few years, other black nurse training schools had opened around the country. In 1894, Daniel Williams was also involved in creating the Freedmen's Hospital and Nurse Training School in Washington, D.C. Under the leadership of Booker T. Washington, the Tuskegee Institute School of Nurse Training in Alabama came into existence in 1892. In the same year, the Hampton Nurse Training School at Dixie Hospital in Hampton, Virginia, began to accept students.

In October 1896, the black women of the **Phyllis Wheatley Club** founded the only black hospital and nurse training school in New Orleans. The Phillis Wheatley Sanitarium and Training School for Nurses began in a private residence, with seven beds and five patients. This institution was later renamed the Flint Goodridge Hospital and Nurse Training School.

On October 4, 1897, Alonzo Clifton McClennan, an 1880 graduate of the **Howard University** Medical School, founded the Hospital and Nursing Training School in Charleston, South Carolina. **Anna De Costa Banks,** one of the first graduates of the Dixie Hospital School of Nursing, became the first head nurse of the South Carolina institution. By 1920, there were thirty-six black nurse training schools.

The schools were founded for a number of reasons, not just to provide training for nurses. McClennan, for example, was angered by the stubborn refusal of the white municipal hospital administrators in Charleston to allow black physicians to attend their patients, even in segregated wards. He and his black colleagues initially created their hospital in order to advance their practices and to care for their patients. They added the nursing school in order to acquire help in bringing medical care to the hordes of poor African Americans of Charleston and the surrounding counties who sought their services.

The black women of the Phyllis Wheatley Club were inspired to establish a nursing school after observing the poor quality of health and the high mortality rates of African Americans in New Orleans. Between 1890 and 1900, the overall death rate in New Orleans dropped from 25.4 to 23.8 per thousand, while that of the city's black population increased from 36.6 to 42.4 per thousand. These conditions were similar in cities both above and below the Mason-Dixon line. The lack of adequate hospital facilities and black health care professionals lessened the already slim chances of survival for African Americans. The establishment of the Phillis Wheatley Sanitarium and Nurse Training School marked the first attempt by African Americans to improve black health care in the city.

Other founders and heads of black nursing schools gave different reasons for starting their schools. Alice Bacon, the white founder of the Hampton Nurse Training School at Dixie Hospital, justified the establishment of the school as a way to keep "in the hands of trained colored women a profession for which, even without training, the Negro women have always shown themselves especially adapted." She declared that black women had "to take up the work laid down by the home-trained women of the old days, and to hold for their race throughout the South a profession that has always been theirs."

Were these early black nursing schools any better than the white schools? Hardly. They were, for the most part, even worse, because black doctors and hospitals were struggling just to get by. Whenever push came to shove, the black nursing students were exploited to make it possible for the facility to survive. They were the fudge factor, the unpaid labor force that took up the slack.

Student nurses performed all the domestic and maintenance drudgery of these institutions. They scrubbed the floors, emptied the bedpans, changed the beds, and did the laundry. They washed patients, sheets, and dishes. This was in addition to tending to the medical needs of patients and dispensing medicine. It's hardly surprising that many student nurses at Tuskegee Institute required extended leaves of absence to recover from damage done to their health while working in the hospital. One of the early Tuskegee catalogs noted that the major admission requirement for entry into the nursing program consisted of a strong physique and much stamina to endure hardship.

The most oppressive aspect of black nursing training at some of these early schools, notably at Tuskegee and Charleston's Nursing Training School, involved the hiring out of student nurses so as to supplement a hospital's income. In the Charleston school, the student nurses were required to turn over to the hospital the dollar a day they earned on private cases. These nurses also managed the hospital's poultry operation, tended the vegetable gardens, and organized public fund-raising activities.

However, in spite of the hardship and the mediocre instruction, hundreds of black women graduated from these segregated hospital nursing programs and went on to render invaluable service to black patients. They survived, they learned, and they went on.

Still, the process of becoming a respected member of the nursing profession involved more than getting the basic training and a diploma. Specialized training or graduate education was also of great importance. And black women were consistently denied admission into many of the country's leading graduate nursing programs.

When black women did manage to get graduate training, their situation did not improve greatly. At every turn, black nurses met with racist attitudes and policies. Challenging career opportunities—such as employment in hospitals, visiting nurse associations, and municipal departments of health—almost always were closed to them. Sympathetic work environments that held out possibilities for promotion to supervisory or administrative positions were out of reach. In fact, the vast majority of black graduate nurses, like their untrained predecessors, worked in private-duty jobs. And they were frequently expected to perform domestic chores in addition to providing nursing care.

Racism was open and blatant. The white superintendent of nurses at the Lincoln Hospital in New York in the early part of the century was asked why there were no black women in supervisory positions at her hospital. She declared without hesitation that "colored" head nurses did not have the capacity to fill positions that entailed heavy responsibility and that discipline could not be maintained unless there was firm, competent white direction.

As bleak as the situation was in the North, the advancement opportunities for

Nursing care in some Southern states was provided by "rural nurses in a movable school truck." This photograph was taken in Madison County, Alabama, in 1923. (NATIONAL ARCHIVES)

black graduate nurses were even more limited in the South. Almost all black graduate nurses in the South worked for lower wages than their white colleagues.

Black nurses had just begun to organize to improve their situation when the world was shaken by war. As their country mobilized to fight, African Americans in the nursing profession saw an opportunity to prove themselves, to show their quality and their commitment. They rushed eagerly to serve . . . and were turned away.

NURSING DURING WORLD WAR I

More than 367,000 black men were called into service during World War I, and, following an effective black protest campaign and lobbying effort, the U.S. Congress authorized the establishment of a separate reserve officers' training camp for black soldiers. Except for the Marine Corps and the pilot section of the aviation corps, black men were permitted to serve in almost every branch of the army and in menial jobs in the navy. Yet black women who fervently desired to use their professional talents and expertise to aid their country during this period were consistently denied the right to serve in the Nurse Corps.

Of all black professionals, women nurses needed no special persuasion to volunteer their services to aid and care for their wounded countrymen. The advent of World War I helped to raise their expectations and excite their professional dreams. Black women nurses desired to seize the opportunity created by the war emergency to accomplish their objectives.

Although the first wave of black women nurses who attempted to enlist in the U.S. Army Nurse Corps expected to encounter racism, they were not prepared for the total rejection of their services during one of America's greatest crises. Disillusioned and hurt, black women nurses initially focused their anger on the American Red Cross, recently reorganized and incorporated by an act of Congress on January 5, 1905.

The Red Cross, an auxiliary of the U.S. Army Nurse Corps, recruited and enrolled nurses, then classified them as First Reserve or Second Reserve nurses. The First Reserve was composed of nurses with the educational, moral, and professional qualifications required by the military nursing corps. The Second Reserve consisted of nurses available for critical civilian nursing who, because of some technicality, such as being over forty years old, were not eligible for the First Reserve. In effect, the American Red Cross enjoyed quasi-governmental status, particularly within the army nursing group. Indeed, the second superintendent of the Nurse Corps, Jane Delano, served simultaneously as head of the Red Cross Nursing Service.

Black nurses demanded to know why so few of them were called or enrolled into either the First or Second Reserve. Delano's response to their inquiries was both evasive and defensive: "We are enrolling colored nurses at the present time," she explained, "and shall continue to do so in order that they may be available if at any time there is an opportunity to assign them to duty in military hospitals." That time and opportunity never seemed to come, and most black nurses waited in vain for the call.

Black nurses in particular, and black Americans in general, felt the injustice deeply. Black criticism of the Red Cross increased as the war continued. The army was markedly reluctant to tap the nursing services of black women, and the navy refused even to consider the matter. As black pressure and anger mounted, the Red Cross belatedly prepared a list of black nurses to serve in a proposed segregated hospital to be established in Des Moines, Iowa. The signing of the armistice on November 11, 1918, and the end of the war, however, aborted the proposed installation. A month before the war's end, though, two dozen black nurses were called for service at Camp Sherman, Ohio; Camp Grant, Illinois; and Camp Sevier, South Carolina.

This number represented only a fraction of the 21,000 white women who had been given the opportunity to serve their country as nurses. Commensurately, as the status of the white nursing profession skyrocketed in the aftermath of the war emergency, that of black nurses plummeted. Because black nurses had not been permitted to serve their country, they apparently could stake no claim to a share of nursing's newly earned public esteem.

THE NACGN AND THE STRUGGLE FOR ACCEPTANCE

Just before the start of World War I, black nurses had begun their long struggle for professional recognition. Besides the injustice of unequal pay, black women graduate nurses considered the denial of membership in the American Nurses Association the most visible and demeaning evidence of professional rejection. Barred from membership in local and state ANA affiliates, the majority of black nurses could not participate in the largest professional association of nurses. And so, in 1908, black nurses took matters into their own hands.

Martha Franklin was the only black student in her graduating class at the Woman's Hospital Training School for Nurses in Philadelphia. That was in 1897. For almost ten years, she encountered daily the inequities, hardships, and injustices faced by black nurses. Then, in the fall of 1906, she began to investigate what her fellow nurses experienced and how they felt about it. She mailed more than 2,000 inquiries to black graduate nurses, superintendents of nursing schools, and nursing organizations to see whether there was any interest in a black society of nurses separate from the ANA.

Her letters struck a responsive chord among the members and leadership of the Lincoln Hospital nursing school. **Adah Belle Thoms**, president of the Lincoln School of Nursing Alumnae Association, arranged a meeting. In August of 1908, fifty-two nurses met at St. Mark's Episcopal Church in New York City to found the **National Association of Colored Graduate Nurses** (NACGN). In 1912, the NACGN members numbered 125, and by 1920, it boasted a membership of 500.

Under the leadership of two of its more forceful presidents, Adah B. Thoms (1915–20) and **Carrie E. Bullock** (1927–30), the NACGN accomplished much. It secured a temporary headquarters in 1918, which consisted of a room in New York City's **Young Women's Christian Association's** 137th Street Branch. In 1920, Thoms filed the NACGN incorporation papers and established a national registry of black graduate nurses to assist them in finding employment.

Bullock focused on two key issues during her tenure. In 1928, in order to facilitate communication and to foster a greater sense of professional involvement among black nurses, she founded and edited the organization's official journal, the *National News Bulletin*. Second, to encourage black women nurses to pursue postgraduate education, Bullock secured the support of managers of the Julius Rosenwald Fund for the establishment of a Rosenwald fellowship program for black graduate nurses.

But this was just a start. Salary inequities in hospitals and public health agencies persisted. Unaccredited black hospital nurse training schools that grossly exploited their students and produced poorly trained nurses continued to multiply. And white nurses remained unresponsive to the entreaties of black women for recognition and acceptance within the nursing profession.

Under the auspices of the Hospital Library and Service Bureau, Donelda Hamlin, in 1925, conducted a survey of state board of health officials and visiting nurse association heads to determine their evaluation and perceptions of black women public health nurses. In her subsequent report, Hamlin emphasized, as representative of the overall response, the comments of the superintendent of the Public Health Nursing Association in Louisville, Kentucky. The respondent declared that "the type of training the average colored nurse received in this part of the country is far inferior to that given to white nurses. Even the best training for colored nurses hardly approximates the poorest training given to white nurses. From another standpoint, their educational background is not so good. Therefore I think the type of service rendered would necessarily be of lower grade than under other circumstances."

In late 1925, the Rockefeller Foundation employed Ethel Johns to examine the status of black women in the nursing profession. Johns visited twenty-three hospitals and nurse training schools for black women during a four-month period. In Chicago, Johns interviewed the chief nurse of the city's health department, which employed ten black graduate nurses and 154 white nurses. She asserted that black nurses' "technique is inferior to that of the white nurses, they are not punctual, and are incapable of analyzing a social situation." She maintained that there was a marked tendency among them "to organize against authority" and "to engage in political intrigue."

Not surprisingly, Johns ended her report on a discouraging if understated note: "Negro nurses in every part of the country feel very keenly that they are debarred from qualifying themselves for leadership and it is true that most doors are closed to them."

In the mid-1930s, the NACGN's situation improved when grants from the

In the 1930s the situation of the National Association of Colored Graduate Nurses improved when grants made it possible to have a permanent headquarters and to hire Mabel Staupers as permanent executive secretary.

General Education Board of the Rockefeller Foundation and from the Julius Rosenwald Fund made it possible for the NACGN to employ **Mabel K. Staupers** as executive secretary and to move into permanent headquarters at Rockefeller Center in New York City, where all the major national nursing organizations had offices. Following a long and relentless struggle, Staupers and NACGN president Estelle Massey Osborne succeeded in winning recognition and acceptance for black nurses.

Staupers' fight to eliminate quotas established by the U.S. Army Nurse Corps

By 1942, when this photograph of nurse Irene Hill was taken in Chicago, the status of black nurses had greatly improved, thanks in part to the efforts of the National Association of Colored Graduate Nurses. (NATIONAL ARCHIVES)

meeting with Eleanor Roosevelt. In November 1944, the first lady and Staupers met, and Staupers described in detail black nurses' troubled relationship with the armed forces.

In January 1945, when Norman T. Kirk announced the possibility of a draft to remedy a nursing shortage within the armed forces, Staupers made a well-publicized response: "If nurses are needed so desperately, why isn't the Army using colored nurses?" Afterward she encouraged nursing groups of all races to write letters and send telegrams protesting the discrimina-

First Lieutenant Nancy C. Leftenant, a graduate of Lincoln Hospital School for Nurses in New York, joined the Reserve Corps of the Army Nurse Corps in February 1945. In March 1948, she became the first black member of the Regular Army Nurse Corps. (MOORLAND-SPINGARN)

constitutes one of the finest periods in NACGN history. Although many black nurses volunteered their services during World War II, they were refused admittance into the navy, and the army allowed only a limited number to serve. In 1943, although the navy had notified Staupers that it had decided to place the induction of black nurses under consideration and the army had raised its quota of black nurses to 160, the situation had not greatly improved.

In an effort to draw attention to the unfairness of quotas, Staupers requested a

Commander Thomas A. Gaylord of the U.S. Navy administers the oath of office on March 8, 1945, to five new navy nurses commissioned in New York. A graduate of Lincoln School for Nurses, Phyllis Mae Daley (second from right) became the first of four black nurses sworn into the Navy Nurse Corps as an ensign. (NATIONAL ARCHIVES)

tion against black nurses in the army and navy nursing corps.

Kirk, Rear Admiral W. J. C. Agnew, and the War Department were soon buried beneath an avalanche of telegrams from an inflamed public, and an end to quotas and exclusion was declared. On January 20, 1945, Kirk stated that nurses would be accepted into the Army Nurse Corps without regard to race, and five days later Agnew announced that the Navy Nurse Corps was open to black women. Within a few weeks, Phyllis Daley became the first black woman to break the color barrier and receive induction into the corps.

The end of discriminatory practices by a key American institution helped to erode entrenched beliefs about the alleged inferiority of black health care professionals and paved the way for the integration of the American Nurses Association. In 1948, the ANA opened its gates to black membership, appointed a black nurse as assistant executive secretary in its national headquarters, and elected **Estelle Osborne** to the board of directors. The decision to grant individual memberships to black nurses barred from state associations in Georgia, Louisiana, South Carolina, Texas, Virginia, Arkansas, Alabama, and the District of Columbia was followed by the adoption of a resolution to establish biracial committees in district and state associations to implement educational programs and promote development of harmonious intergroup relations.

With the removal of the overtly discriminatory barriers to membership in the ANA, members of the NACGN recognized that their needs would now be served by the ANA, which agreed to take over the functions of the NACGN and to continue to award the Mary Mahoney Medal honoring individuals for their contributions to interracial understanding. Thus, during the NACGN's 1949 convention, the members voted the organization out of existence, and the following year, Staupers, then president, presided over its formal dissolution.

NINETEENTH-CENTURY PHYSICIANS

If black nurses faced such overwhelming obstacles, what was life like for a black woman who hoped to become a doctor? Almost all colleges and universities were closed to women, black and white. The doors to medical schools were shut even tighter. In 1849, a white woman named Elizabeth Blackwell had battled her way into and through a small rural medical school in west central New York to become the first woman doctor in the United States or Britain.

In 1864, fifteen years after Elizabeth Blackwell became the first American woman medical graduate, the first black woman graduate, **Rebecca Lee [Crumpler]**, received a doctor of medicine degree from the New England Female Medical College in Boston. Three years later, the second black American woman physician, **Rebecca J. Cole**, graduated from the Woman's Medical College of Pennsylvania. In 1870, **Susan Smith McKinney Steward** completed her studies at New York Medical College for Women. Lee, Cole, and Steward signaled the emergence of black women in the medical profession.

Black women physicians such as Rebecca J. Cole skillfully combined private medical practice with community service among white and black women. Cole worked for a time with Elizabeth and Emily Blackwell at the New York Infirmary for Women and Children as a "sanitary visitor." The infirmary's Tenement House Service, begun in 1866, was the earliest practical program of medical social service in the country. As a sanitary visitor or tenement physician, Cole made house calls in slum neighborhoods, teaching indigent mothers the basics of hygiene and "the preservation of health of their families." Elizabeth Blackwell described Cole as "an intelligent young coloured physician" who conducted her work "with tact and care" and thus demonstrated that the establishment of a social service department "would be a valuable addition to every hospital."

The late nineteenth century witnessed a dramatic increase in the number of women doctors in America. In 1860, there were about 200. Twenty years later, in 1880, there were 2,423, more than ten times as many. By 1900, that number had tripled, to more than 7,000.

During this forty-year period, nineteen medical schools for women were founded. By 1895, eleven of them had disbanded, but by that time a small number of men's medical schools were admitting an occasional woman student.

Black women at first seemed to benefit from these new opportunities for women in medicine. In the twenty-five years after the ending of slavery, and during the height of racial segregation and discrimination, there were 115 black women physicians in the United States. However, by the 1920s, the U.S. Census listed only sixty-five black women as practicing physicians.

Not surprisingly, black male physicians far outnumbered their female counterparts. In 1890, there were 909 black male physicians, and by 1920 the number had jumped to 3,885. The increase was due largely to the existence of several medical schools founded for African Americans in the post–Reconstruction South. By 1914, however, of the approved black medical schools, only Howard and Meharry remained open. These two institutions played the most significant role in the education of black women physicians during that period.

The Howard University Medical School was chartered in 1868, and was supported by the U.S. government as an institution to train African Americans. By 1900, it had graduated 552 physicians, twenty-five of whom were black women.

Meharry Medical College graduated the largest number of black women physicians (thirty-nine by 1920). Originally the Department of Medicine at Central Tennessee College in 1876, Meharry was the first medical school in the South to provide for the education of black physicians. Meharry's location in the South made it the logical place for the majority of black women to pursue a medical education. In 1893, seventeen years after its opening, Meharry graduated its first black women physicians, Annie D. Gregg and Georgiana Esther Lee Patton. The first woman to teach at Meharry and attain a position of leadership as superintendent of Hubbard Hospital was Josie E. Wells, a member of the class of 1904.

By the turn of the century, the Woman's Medical College of Pennsylvania, established in 1850 as the first regular medical school for women, had graduated approximately a dozen black women physicians. This institution blazed a new trail by providing medical training to women of every race, creed, and national origin. Indeed, all of the women's medical colleges, which in most instances were founded as temporary expediencies, enabled women to escape social ostracism, subtle discrimination, and overt hostility throughout their training in a male-dominated profession. However, the trend toward coeducation in the 1870s did not result in an increase in the percentage of black women physicians. Only one or two black women attended the integrated coeducational institutions.

Among the early black women graduates of the Woman's Medical College were Rebecca J. Cole (1867), **Caroline Still Wiley Anderson** (1878), **Verina Morton Jones** (1888), **Halle Tanner Dillon Johnson** (1891), **Lucy Hughes Brown** (1894), **Alice Woodby-McKane** (1894), **Matilda Arabella Evans** (1897), and **Eliza Anna Grier** (1897). Three of these graduates—Johnson, Jones, and Brown—became the first black women to practice medicine in Alabama, Mississippi, and South Carolina, respectively. The successes achieved by the Woman's Medical College's black graduates possibly attest to a high quality of education and underscore the advantage of providing a more nurturing and supportive all-woman environment in which students may learn from female faculty role models.

The majority of early black women physicians were the daughters of socially privileged black families or others who, perhaps to protect them from menial labor or domestic servitude, encouraged their daughters to educate themselves. That family background and prior education were important determinants of success in acquiring a medical education is reflected in the lives of a few of the early black women physicians.

Caroline Anderson was the daughter of William Still, a founder of the Underground Railroad, chairman of the General Vigilance Committee in antebellum Philadelphia, and author of *The Underground Railroad* (1872), which chronicled the escape of runaway slaves. Halle Johnson was the daughter of Bishop B. T. Tanner of the African Methodist Episcopal Church in Philadelphia. Susan Steward was the daughter of a prosperous Brooklyn, New York, merchant. Sarah Logan Fraser's father was Bishop Logan of the Zion Methodist Episcopal Church in Syracuse, New York. Like William Still, Bishop Logan had aided and harbored escaping slaves in his home. Unlike Anderson, Johnson, and Steward, Fraser received her medical degree from the Medical School of Syracuse University, rather than the Woman's Medical College.

Sarah G. Boyd Jones' father, George W. Boyd, was reputed to be the wealthiest black man in Richmond. Sarah Jones attended the Richmond Normal School before completing her medical training in 1893 at Howard University Medical School. After graduation she returned to Richmond, where she became the first woman to pass the Virginia medical board examinations. She later founded the Richmond Hospital and Training School of Nurses, which in 1902 was renamed the Sarah G. Jones Memorial Hospital.

To be sure, not all of the first generation of black women physicians belonged to illustrious families. Some, such as Eliza Grier, were former slaves who worked their way through college and medical school, occasionally receiving limited financial assistance from parents or siblings. In 1890, Grier wrote to the Woman's Medical College concerning her financial straits: "I have not money and no source from which to get it only as I work for every dollar. . . . What I want to know from you is this. How much does it take to put one through a year in your school? Is there any possible chance to do any work that would not interfere with one's studies?" Grier apparently completed the medical program by working every other year, since she graduated seven years later, in 1897.

Black women who were fortunate enough to receive medical education encountered additional obstacles after graduation. Racial customs and negative attitudes toward women dictated that black women physicians practice almost exclusively among African Americans, and primarily among black women, many of whom avoided treatment since the payment of medical fees was a great hardship. Poverty was often accompanied by superstition and fear. Consequently, new black women doctors frequently had to expend considerable effort persuading, cajoling, and winning confidence before being allowed to treat physical illness.

It is significant that many black women who were able to establish private practices also founded hospitals, nurse training schools, and social service agencies. Since black professionals and patients were prohibited from or segregated within local health care facilities, these black institutions became crucial to their practices and to the welfare of the black community.

Several black graduates of the Woman's Medical College, most notably Lucy Brown and Matilda Evans, established such institutions. After her 1894 graduation, Brown took up practice in Charleston, South Carolina. In 1896, she joined a small group of eight black male physicians led by Alonzo C. McClellan and established the Hospital and Nursing Training School in Charleston. Evans moved to Columbia, South Carolina, in 1897, where she practiced medicine for twenty years. Since there were no hospital facilities open to African Americans in the city, Evans initially cared for patients in her own home. Eventually, as her number of clients grew, she was able to rent a separate building with facilities for thirty patients, and she established a full-scale hospital and nurse training school. She also founded the Negro Health Association of South Carolina.

Other black women physicians accepted appointments as resident physicians in segregated black colleges and universities established in the South during Reconstruction. Such appointments provided small but steady stipends and much-needed experience at working in an institutional setting. Moreover, they assured a degree of professional autonomy, status, and visibility, and enabled the development of greater self-confidence.

During the 1890s and early 1900s, Halle Johnson, **Ionia R. Whipper,** Verina Jones, and Susan Steward became resident physicians at black colleges. Not only did they minister to the health care needs of the college students and faculty, but they often taught courses and lectured on health subjects. Johnson served as the first black woman resident physician at Tuskegee Institute from 1891 to 1894. She was responsible for the medical care of 450 students as well as for thirty officers and teachers and their families. She was expected to make her own medicines, and she taught one or two classes each term. For her efforts she was paid $600 per year plus room and board and was allowed one month of vacation.

In 1903, Ionia R. Whipper, a member of the 1903 graduating class of Howard Medical School, succeeded Johnson as resident physician at Tuskegee Institute. However, by this time, there had been a change in attitudes toward women, a step backward. Whipper was restricted to the care of female students at the institute.

After leaving Tuskegee, Whipper returned to Washington, D.C., where she and a group of seven friends established a home for unwed, pregnant, school-age black girls, initially in her own home. In 1931, she purchased property and opened the Ionia R. Whipper Home for Unwed Mothers, which had a policy of nondiscrimination as to race, religion, or residence.

After completing her education at the Woman's Medical College, Verina Jones accepted an appointment as resident physician of Rust College in Holly Springs, Mississippi. Like Johnson and Whipper, she doubled as a teacher, conducting classes at the industrial school connected with the university.

Like their white women counterparts, black women physicians remained sensitive to the prevailing social attitude that higher education and professional training threatened a woman's femininity. However, since economic necessity and racism so limited the opportunities of black men that black women, regardless of marital status, had to contribute to the well-being of the family, black Americans were more tolerant of women working outside the home.

Indeed, the black woman physician was frequently a much sought-after marriage partner. Many black women physicians married black ministers, physicians, or educators. Susan Steward, commenting on the marriageability of these women, has observed: "Fortunate are the men who marry these women from an economic standpoint at least. They are blessed in a three-fold measure, in that they take unto themselves a wife, a trained nurse, and a doctor." Furthermore, since nineteenth-century medical practices were frequently located in the home, marriage and career could be conducted in the same place.

These early physicians were remarkable women, as were those black women who followed after them. They were committed, self-reliant, and talented, of course. They had to be. They were also aware of their place in history and their responsibility to the black community. In this, they were not alone. Other black women who were more accustomed to afternoon tea than to midnight shifts worked beside them to provide health care to all African Americans.

CLUBWOMEN AND THEIR INSTITUTIONS

Although they were not health professionals, the members of black women's clubs were crucial contributors to the history of health and medicine in the black community during this time. They were major fund-raisers for hospitals and schools, and they were often founders of health care institutions.

The women of the Woman's Improvement Club of Indianapolis are a case in point. Founded in 1903 as a literary club, the group soon became involved in the question of care for black tuberculosis patients. The club members studied medical manuals and talked to doctors to determine what would be most useful and decided on a tuberculosis camp. They then went out into the business community and into the churches to raise money. By 1905, they had opened the Oak Hill Tuberculosis Camp.

By 1911, the club had established a system of referrals to the camp with nurses from the Metropolitan Life Insurance Company. They also sponsored tuberculosis education meetings at which representatives of the Marion County Tuberculosis Society and the Marion County Board of Health spoke and gave instruction. And by 1916, the Woman's Improvement Club was supplying county health officials with statistics about tuberculosis in the black community. They also helped open a publicly funded health clinic in the community. In 1918, a lobbying effort by the club resulted in added bed space for black patients at Sunnyside Sanitarium and a new ward at Flower Mission Hospital.

Between 1922 and 1928, the club founded and operated its own hospital for tuberculosis patients. Their contribution to health care for the black community of their city was remarkable. And they were not alone. Other black women's clubs around the country made similar contributions.

A major area of club involvement was in care for the aged. The **Woman's Loyal Union** founded the Home for Aged Colored People in Brooklyn and the New Bedford Home for the Aged. Detroit's Phyllis Wheatley Home for Aged Colored Women was founded by the Phyllis Wheatley Club of that city. The Alpha Home in Indianapolis, the Cleveland Home for Aged Colored People, and other facilities in Chicago, Newark, New Haven, and Philadelphia were founded by individual women and then supported by women's clubs.

Hospitals were also high on the clubwomen's agendas. Berean Church clubwomen helped Dr. Caroline Still Anderson establish a dispensary in Philadelphia. The Yates Women's Club in Cairo, Illinois, supported a small black hospital in that town. And, of course, clubs around the country raised funds for established black hospitals.

In 1935, in the midst of the Great Depression, the **Alpha Kappa Alpha Sorority** established the Mississippi Health Project. Several mobile health units were staffed by twelve visiting doctors, nurses, and other health care providers. They traveled 5,324 miles in one summer, immunizing more than 2,000 children against diphtheria and smallpox, giving medical attention of various kinds to 2,267 rural African Americans, and distributing 6,800 health pamphlets. The project continued, and expanded, for eight years. The surgeon general of the U.S. Public Health Service, Thomas Parren, called it one of the finest jobs of volunteer public health work he had ever seen.

This work went far beyond the traditional "good deeds" of women's clubs in general. There was a special consciousness behind the efforts of black women, an awareness that they were serving their own people and that no one else was going to. The work of these groups formed the basis of a powerful new movement.

NATIONAL NEGRO HEALTH MOVEMENT

In 1914, Monroe Nathan Work, a sociologist at Tuskegee Institute, provided an alarming statistical analysis of black Americans' health in the South. His calculations indicated that nearly half of all black deaths were premature. His findings moved Tuskegee's founder, Booker T. Washington, to begin thinking about a national movement to improve the health of African Americans.

The Negro Organization Society of Virginia also played a major role in providing the foundation for the National Negro Health Movement. Under the direction of Robert Russa Moton in 1912, this organization started day-long campaigns to clean up the farms and neighborhoods in Virginia. With the support of the Virginia Board of Health, the campaign expanded to a week.

Then, in 1915, Washington initiated a Health Improvement Week at Tuskegee Institute. This became National Negro Health Week (NNHW). Sixteen states participated during the first year. Lectures at schools and churches, distribution of health pamphlets, and special cleanup services took place across the country. This observance brought national attention to the black health care crisis, and it would become the catalyst for the National Negro Health Movement, officially launched in 1932.

After Washington died on November 14, 1915, plans for a National Negro Health Week in 1916 did not materialize. In 1917, however, under the leadership of Tuskegee faculty Moton and Work, Washington's efforts were renewed and the institutionalization of NNHW began.

It was decided that Booker T. Washington would be honored as founder of the movement by celebrating National Negro Health Week during the first week in April, to commemorate his birth on April 5. Also, the week would be expanded into a year-round program. Health leaders concluded that the best way to do this would be to get the U.S. Public Health Service (USPHS) to take over NNHW.

In 1932, NNHW came under the purview of the USPHS, and this branch of the government became the center for all activity concerning black health issues. The name National Negro Health Movement was coined, and the USPHS opened the Office of Negro Health Work under the direction of Dr. Roscoe C. Brown. Activities sparked by NNHW survived well into the 1940s, and were supported by minority and nonminority associations and public health departments. Various health educa-

tion and special clinical services were sponsored nationwide. During this time, Dr. Brown kept records of participation throughout the country. He reported that the number of people reached through NNHW increased from 500,000 in 1933 to 5,000,000 in 1942. These figures suggest it was indeed a mass movement.

From 1932 to 1950, a quarterly newsletter chronicling the movement, the *National Negro Health News,* was published. In 1950, the USPHS declared the end of the black health program and closed the NNHW office. Although the health status of African Americans had improved significantly, a two-tiered health care system remained, one for white Americans and one for black Americans.

MEDICINE IN THE TWENTIETH CENTURY

The two-headed monster of sexism and racism has loomed over medicine well into the twentieth century. As being a doctor became more profitable and prestigious, those in control of the profession tightened their grip.

Dr. **Dorothy Ferebee,** a 1924 honors graduate of Tufts University Medical School, accurately described the challenges faced by twentieth-century black women physicians when, discussing her years at Tufts, she noted: "It was not easy. The medical school had five women out of 137 students. We women were always the last to get assignments in amphitheaters and clinics. And I? I was the last of the last because not only was I a woman, but a Negro, too." Yet, the history of these women also reveals that despite these barriers, they have advanced in and made important contributions to their profession.

Only a small number of black women have become physicians. In 1920, sixty-five black women practiced medicine. Fifty years later, the number had increased to 1,051. By 1989, the number had grown to 3,250, but this represented less than 1 percent of the practicing physicians in the United States. Until the advent of affirmative action programs in the 1970s, most black women graduated from the two predominantly black medical schools, Howard University and Meharry Medical College. Indeed, the doors of most medical schools in the United States were closed to *all women* until the early 1960s.

But admission to medical school, difficult as it was, paled beside an even more overwhelming obstacle. In contrast to their nineteenth-century counterparts, twentieth-century black women physicians had to gain access to hospitals. Hospitals had become essential to medical education, medical practice, and medical specialization. Several states had even passed laws requiring the completion of an internship as a prerequisite for a medical license.

These changes in medical practice threatened the future of black physicians and placed an additional burden on black women's advancement in the profession. African-American physicians seeking internships and residencies were expected to pursue them at black hospitals, which usually had inferior programs. Moreover, black hospitals preferred to admit black men, and the few women's hospitals did not always welcome black women.

The opportunities, therefore, for black women to obtain hospital appointments and specialty training were severely limited. Isabella Vandervall, a 1915 graduate of the New York Medical College for Women, was rejected for an internship by four hospitals, including the one affiliated with her medical school. No one could say she was unqualified. She had graduated first in her class. The problem was simply and straightforwardly a question of race and gender. Fortunately, she was able to practice, having obtained licenses in New York and New Jersey before the laws on compulsory internship had gone into effect.

In 1923, Lillian Atkins Moore, a senior medical student at Woman's Medical College of Pennsylvania, applied for an internship at the college's hospital. She too was rejected because she was black. The hospital's medical director admitted that race had been the deciding factor in the hospital's action and offered to get her an appointment at one of the "colored" hospitals. Moore finally secured a position at Douglass Hospital, a black hospital in Philadelphia.

A few black women were able to gain admission to programs at government hospitals. Dorothy Ferebee, after several rejections from white hospitals, secured an internship at Freedmen's Hospital in Washington, D.C. In 1926, **May Chinn** became the first black woman intern at Harlem Hospital.

This was not the first time that Chinn had been a pioneer. She was also the first black woman to graduate from Bellevue Hospital Medical College. She soon found that racial discrimination prohibited black physicians from gaining appointments to private hospitals. Therefore Chinn was forced during the 1930s to perform major surgery in patients' homes. In her autobiography, she compared the situation to practicing medicine in the isolated hills of Appalachia a hundred years earlier.

Margaret Lawrence also completed her internship at Harlem Hospital. She had not been allowed to work at New York's Babies' Hospital because, according to the hospital, housing could not be provided for a black woman in the nurses' dormitory. The nurses' dormitory, of course, was where women interns were housed. The white women were segregated from other doctors, and the black women were segregated from the white women.

This was not the first time that Lawrence encountered racial barriers. When she arrived at Cornell University in 1932, Lawrence was the only black undergraduate on campus and was not allowed to live in the dorms. She supported herself by working as a domestic for white families. Nonetheless, she did well academically and expected to be admitted to Cornell Medical School. She was not admitted, however, and was told that it was because a black man who had been admitted twenty-five years earlier had contracted tuberculosis. Lawrence eventually gained admission to Columbia Medical School and, once again, was the only black student. In 1946, she became the first black trainee at the Columbia Psychoanalytic Clinic.

Racism was not the only obstacle encountered along the professional paths of twentieth-century black women physicians. When Chinn first went into practice in Harlem, she encountered resistance from her black male colleagues. She later noted that they appeared to be divided into three distinct groups. "The first group," she stated, "didn't believe that a woman should be a doctor, so they pretended that I didn't

exist. The second group actively discouraged patients from coming to me: 'What can she do for you that a man cannot do better?' The third group said they were helping me by sending me on their night calls after midnight."

Margaret Lawrence also had to battle sexism. At Meharry Medical College during the early 1940s, she was the only woman on the faculty and encountered blatant sexism. She was excluded from intellectual camaraderie, overburdened with responsibilities, and poorly paid in comparison with her male colleagues.

Still, an examination of the work of twentieth-century black women physicians demonstrates the significant contributions that they have made to medicine and their communities. These women founded hospitals, established civic organizations, practiced medicine among the underserved, and challenged barriers in a profession that has been and continues to be white and male dominated.

Matilda Evans, the first black woman to practice in South Carolina, established three hospitals between 1898 and 1916. In 1930, she established a free clinic for mothers and children in the basement of a black church. **Virginia Alexander,** a 1925 graduate of Woman's Medical College of Pennsylvania, established the Aspiranto Health Home in 1931 to provide health care for poor women and children in North Philadelphia. She also worked as a civil rights activist. Dorothy Ferebee directed the Alpha Kappa Alpha Mississippi Health Project, which had been designed by the sorority to bring much-needed health care to the poor of the Mississippi Delta every summer from 1935 to 1942.

Throughout most of the twentieth century, most black women physicians had general practices because of their limited opportunities to obtain specialty training. Since World War II, more have entered the more prestigious and financially rewarding medical specialties. In 1946, **Helen O. Dickens,** the daughter of a former slave, received her certification from the American Board of Obstetrics and Gynecology. Four years later, she became the first black woman admitted to the American College of Surgeons. The American Board of Surgery certified its first black woman, Hughenna L. Gauntlett, in 1968, and the American Board of Neurological Surgery certified its first, **Alexa Canady,** in 1984.

Black women have also begun to assume leadership roles within the profession. In 1958, Edith Irby Jones broke the racial barriers of Southern medical schools when she became the first black person, male or female, admitted to the University of Arkansas School of Medicine. In 1985, Jones became the first woman president of the National Medical Association, a predominantly black medical society. By 1991, two other black women, Vivian Pinn-Wiggins and Alma R. George, had headed the organization.

In 1991, Pinn-Wiggins was appointed the first permanent director of the National Institutes of Health Office of Women's Health Research. **Roselyn Payne Epps,** in 1990, became the first black physician to be president of the American Medical Women's Association. Despite these achievements, only a few black women have assumed prominent roles in the medical hierarchy. Few have been named department chairs and none has been named a medical school dean.

In their pursuit of medical careers, twentieth-century black women physicians have had to challenge stereotypical notions about black women and their work. Chinn once recalled that a black woman patient wept as Chinn approached her because "she felt she had been denied the privilege of having a white doctor wait on her." While Margaret Lawrence was in medical school, white women often stopped her on the street to offer her work as a maid.

The tenacity of these stereotypes about black women and their work lingers. Even in the late twentieth century, black women medical students are at times assumed to be members of the cleaning staff. For nurses, too, the struggle for equality has continued into the present day.

The fight for integration into state nurses' associations in the South continued even after the ANA openly accepted black members. **Mary Elizabeth Lancaster Carnegie** led the attack against the Florida State Nurses Association (FSNA). Her description of the black nurses' struggle for the right to participate in the meetings of the FSNA illuminates the strength of their determination to win professional recognition and acceptance. It also shows the absurd nature of the efforts of some white nurses to preserve segregation and subordination.

"For many months," Carnegie explains, "we played a game of 'musical chairs.' The white nurses would wait on the outside of the buildings for us to arrive and be seated; then they would proceed to sit on the opposite side of the meeting room. If we sat in the back, they would sit in the front, and vice versa." Carnegie devised a clever scheme to end "the game." She and her fellow black nurses simply waited for the white nurses to arrive and then scattered throughout the room. If the white nurses wanted to sit down, they had to sit near *somebody* black.

When, in 1950, Carnegie was elected to the association's board for a three-year term, she continued to press quietly for integration. After the 1950 meeting Carnegie observed that "for the first time, all Negro nurses attended all business and program meetings, but [they were still] barred from the luncheon.

By the time of the 1952 convention in Daytona Beach, Florida, Carnegie was able to report modest improvements. "There was integration in every respect but housing," she said, "and the events that were strictly social." The luncheon meetings at the hotel included all members on an equal basis.

By the 1950s, it had become evident that the self-image of black nurses was formed in part by the twin realities of racism and sexism in American society. Black nurses recognized that their struggle for recognition, acceptance, and equality of opportunity within the nursing field was inextricably linked to the fight to blunt this double-edged prejudice. Carnegie's words capture the relationship between the development of a positive self-image and the struggle for unfettered access to professional opportunities: "In the length and breadth of the United State of America, Negro nurses, many unknown to each other, have always fought for a common cause. . . . They were fighting on the same front in schools of nursing and in professional organizations in other states, and on other fronts—in the military, public health, hospital nursing service, industry, private duty, and the national organizations—throughout the country."

Actually, the dual process of working with and against the system allowed black nurses to develop a collective pride and self-esteem in the face of the oppression they endured. Central to their identity was a strong conviction that, in the words of black nurse educator-administrator Gloria R. Smith, "black nurses were accountable to black people in a special way."

In 1971, black nurses found it desirable again to organize in a separate body to continue the fight for full participation in and equal access to opportunities in the profession. The creation of the new National Black Nurses Association reminds us of the resiliency of negative images, racism, discrimination . . . and of the will to overcome injustices of all kinds.

That same will has been tested even more severely in scientific fields outside health and medicine. While, in medicine, black women often have had to slip in through the back door, in other areas of science they have often remained firmly shut out. Still, they have made their contributions whenever and wherever they could. Doubtless, history has probably failed to record most of them, but some have come down to us. And others are only now being made.

INVENTORS

Inventors are the mavericks of science. To them, problems are like Mount Everest—there to be tackled. Often they work with few resources beyond their own creativity and intelligence. Many are self-educated. But their peculiar combination of intense practicality and unbounded imagination make them among the most fascinating of all scientists.

Women inventors have often been overlooked in the history of invention. The word *inventor* itself has acquired a masculine overtone, and reference works use exclusively the inventions of men as examples of the act or process of inventing. Yet there have been women inventors throughout American history. As early as 1715, patents were granted by the British government to Thomas Masters for "a new invention found out by Sybilla, his wife, for cleaning and curing the Indian Corn growing in the several colonies in America," and in 1809 Mary Kies, another white woman, received a U.S. patent for a process of weaving silk.

African-American women have been successful in this field, demonstrating creativity and problem-solving skills that have been recognized by U.S. patents over the years. There have been obstacles, however. Just as African-American men often faced discrimination in getting their new ideas tried and accepted, so did these women face the obstacle of race. In addition, they confronted discrimination against women in a domain that, because it required mechanical and technical skills, was thought to be for men only. Because they were not expected or encouraged to be interested in technology, women were generally excluded from studies and opportunities in this field.

African-American women, then, had three hurdles to overcome: resistance to new ideas (one that all inventors face); discrimination because of race; and discrimination because of gender. Added to all this is the cost of patenting, which may involve making a model or having drawings made by a draftsperson. It seems certain that many talented black women have not had the financial resources to complete applications for patents.

Lacking the mechanical or technical apprenticeships, training, and experience available to men, women have had to rely on creative spirits and the determination to turn ideas for solving problems into the solutions themselves. Not infrequently, they have been unable to exploit their inventions to the fullest.

Ellen Elgin is an example. In the 1880s, Elgin, who lived in Washington, D.C., and was a member of the Women's National Industrial League, invented a clothes-wringer. She sold her invention to an agent for $18, and he manufactured it. The clothes-wringer was a success, and Elgin was asked why she had sold it so cheaply. She had, after all, devoted years of time to its development. Elgin replied that she was afraid that if it was known to be the invention of a black woman, the wringer would not be bought by white women.

While the number of recorded inventions by African-American women is small, the variety is impressive, ranging from domestic items to complex mechanical devices to health aids.

Between 1885 and 1898, five African-American women received U.S. patents. The first was Sara E. Goode, owner of a Chicago furniture store. Goode designed a "Folding Cabinet Bed," similar to today's sofa bed or convertible. The second patent awarded to an African-American woman went to Miriam E. Benjamin in 1888 for a "Gong and Signal Chair" for hotels. This chair was adopted by the U.S. House of Representatives for signaling pages.

Four years after Benjamin received her patent, Anna Mangin of Woodside, New

York, patented an improved pastry fork. In that same year, a patent was awarded to Sarah Boone of New Haven, Connecticut, for an improved ironing board.

Among the inventions that were patented by African-American women in the next half century were an "Apparatus for Holding Yarn Skeins" (Julia F. Hammonds), a hair brush that permitted easy cleaning (Lydia D. Newman), a fruit press for extracting juice (Madeline Turner), a form of central heating (Alice H. Parker), and a permanent wave machine (Marjorie S. Joyner).

In 1945, Henrietta Bradbury broke new ground, going well beyond the areas of "women's work." She developed a "Torpedo Discharge Means" using compressed air.

The most prolific African-American woman inventor to date is Mary B. D. Kenner, who patented five inventions between 1956 and 1987, devices ranging from health aids to household conveniences. "It [invention] runs in my family," Kenner has said. "Both my father and grandfather were inventors, so I inherited it." Kenner's sister Mildred A. Smith is also an inventor. She received a patent grant in 1980 for a game that teaches family relationships and history.

In the 1960s and 1970s, African-American women invented, among other things, a home security system (Marie Van Brittan Brown), an attachment for rotary floor washers that cleans corners and baseboards (Gertrude Downing), and a pain reliever (Mary A. Moore).

In 1980, Valerie Thomas received a patent for her "Illusion Transmitter." Her invention is a "three-dimensional illusional television-like system for transmitting an illusion of an object" before your eyes. Thomas has a degree in physics from Morgan State University and is a data analyst for the National Aeronautics and Space Administration. On the job, she has worked on the development of the Landsat image-processing systems for more than ten years. The sophistication of her invention reflects the training she has received and is clear evidence of a changing situation. Even though African-American women have been inventing social and political tools for hundreds of years, their efforts to create new material realities are only just beginning to be recognized.

SCIENCE IN THE TWENTIETH CENTURY

In 1876, Edward A. Bouchet became the first black man to earn a doctorate in the United States, graduating from Yale University with a degree in physics. One hundred years later, in 1976, **Shirley A. Jackson** became the first black woman in the United States to earn a doctorate in physics, from the Massachusetts Institute of Technology (MIT). This century-long gap between Bouchet and Jackson reflects the very different experiences of black men and black women in the sciences in this country.

In few other professions has the gap between black male and female participation been so great. From 1876 to 1940, only ninety black people earned doctorates in the sciences—95 percent of the recipients were male, and 5 percent were female. These pioneering black women scientists included Ruth E. Moore (bacteriology,

Ohio State University, 1933), Jessie Jarue Mark (botany, Iowa State University, 1935), Flemmie P. Kittrell (nutrition, Cornell University, 1936), **Roger Arliner Young** (zoology, University of Pennsylvania, 1940), and Ruth Lloyd (anatomy, Western Reserve University, 1941). In contrast, by 1940 more than 25,000 white men and 2,000 white women held doctorates in the sciences.

From the late nineteenth century until 1940, black women who wanted to become scientists had to face two huge obstacles.

First, few women of any color were allowed to enter educational institutions in which they could be trained as scientists. Science was, quite routinely, considered as being beyond the capabilities of the female mind. In Britain, women were excluded from the Royal Society of Science. In France, they were excluded from the Academy of Science.

However, after Marie Curie was awarded the Nobel prize *twice* and was still being kept out of the Academy, some male scientists began to wonder whether

Spelman College was one of the few institutions that routinely provided science education for black women. Depicted here is a chemistry class. (SPELMAN COLLEGE ARCHIVES)

they were being a little unjust. "All academies tend to be conservative and move
slowly," said a writer for the magazine
Nature in 1911. . . . They were created
by men for men and for the most part at a
time when women played little or no part
in those occupations which such societies
were intended to foster and develop. But
the times have changed. Women have grad-
ually won for themselves their rightful positions as human beings. We have now to
recognize that academies as seats of learning were made for humanity and that, as
members of the human race, women have
the right to look upon their heritage and
property no less than men."

This bold statement was followed by a
qualification. "This consummation may
not at once be reached," said the writer,
"but, as it is based upon reason and justice,
it is certain to be attained eventually." As
it turns out, "eventually" has been a long
time in coming.

For example, almost all of the women
who managed to get doctorates in science
ended up teaching in women's colleges. In
the years 1900 to 1920, according to a
study by Margaret Rossiter, only 9 percent
of women physicists were employed outside of women's colleges. And, not surprisingly, physics laboratories in women's
colleges were not equipped to enable
groundbreaking research.

For black women, the prejudice against
women was compounded by the economic
and educational situation of African
Americans. The few black women pursuing
the sciences during this period were largely
educated at the undergraduate level in the
historically black colleges in the South.
These colleges had even fewer of the resources needed for the training of scientists,

such as laboratory equipment, advanced
courses, or extensive library holdings, than
women's colleges did.

Furthermore, many educators at these
colleges did not view science as a viable
occupation for black students because few
scientific institutions employed black graduates. These same educators also felt that
black women should train to be teachers,
for which there was a critical need in black
communities. However, the biggest barrier
faced by all black people who wanted to
study science in this period was the belief
held by many white scientists that, as
W. E. B. DuBois put it: "the exact and
intensive habit of mind, the rigorous mathematical logic demanded of those who
would be scientists is not natural to the
Negro race."

Against this background, the few black
women who managed to earn doctorates
in the sciences were unique and committed
women. Those who succeeded had to overcome stereotypes as to appropriate wom-
en's roles both within and outside their
communities, as well as the prejudice of
white scientists. Typically they pursued
their scientific careers in institutions that
required them to teach a great deal, thus
allowing them little time for research. It is
not surprising that all of these first black
women scientists earned degrees in the biological sciences, the fields most open to
women in general in this period.

After 1940—and especially after World
War II—scientific institutions in the United
States experienced a tremendous growth.
The successful use of sophisticated technology such as radar during the war fueled
the growth of many new industries in the
postwar era. Surely the most visible sign
of the new spirit of scientific development

emerged in the 1960s with the drive to put a person on the moon. Expanded employment opportunities for scientists, coupled with the breakdown of laws supporting racial segregation, made it possible for many more black women to pursue careers in the sciences.

Black women began to earn degrees in many fields, among them mathematics (**Marjorie Lee Browne,** University of Michigan, 1949, and **Evelyn Boyd Granville,** Yale, 1949), geology (Margurite Thomas, Catholic University, 1942), chemical engineering (Jenny Patrick, MIT, 1979), and mechanical engineering (**Christine Darden,** George Washington University, 1983). These women have had successful careers as educators and researchers. In addition, they have served as positive role models, encouraging young black women to prepare themselves for careers in science.

In 1973, for example, Shirley Ann Jackson became the first black woman to earn a Ph.D. from the Massachusetts Institute of Technology (MIT). A physicist, Jackson went to work at the Fermi National Accelerator Laboratory, working on elemental particle theories. After a year at Fermi and one at the European Center for Nuclear Research in Geneva, Switzerland, she joined AT&T's Bell Laboratories.

From her position at AT&T, Jackson has been able to influence the opportunities in science for other black women. She has served on the New Jersey Commission on Science and Technology, committees of the National Academy of Science, the American Association for the Advancement of Science, and the National Science Foundation.

Other black women scientists have chosen to move away from teaching and research altogether to work full time on expanding opportunities for others. Marian Johnson-Thompson had just been awarded a $338,000 grant to continue her research on multidrug resistance when she was asked to join the National Institute for Environmental Health Sciences staff as a minority recruiter. She wasn't sure what to think. "I never wanted to be a paper pusher," she said in an interview with *Science* magazine. "I was concerned about trading off academic freedom for a position where ultimately you speak for the president. My students didn't want me to leave." However, Johnson-Thompson decided to take the job. "When you get to a certain age," she said, "you start thinking about where you can make the biggest impact."

A lot of other black scientists have made the same kind of decision. In fact, according to the National Science Foundation (NSF), 21 percent of black Ph.D. scientists and engineers were working in administration in 1989, as compared to 17 percent of white scientists and engineers. These people are making policy about how science is taught, how minorities are treated, and what government guidelines will be for the health and welfare of the nation.

They are working at the National Institutes of Health (NIH), and the National Aeronautics and Space Administration (NASA). One black woman, **Joycelyn Elders,** was named Surgeon General in 1993, and another, Hazel O'Leary, became Secretary of Energy the same year.

These are important and powerful positions. At the same time, there is some concern that black women, along with other minorities, are going into administration because they are being shut out of hands-on research. And there is certainly no doubt that the "old boy" network is particularly strong in science. It is also particularly destructive, because of the way scientific knowledge progresses.

At any given time, the most important research being done is shared, not just through publications and publicly read papers, but through "scientific friendships" between researchers who may be separated by a continent, an ocean, or even half a world. They, and their graduate students and protégés, share information and resources on a regular basis. A scientist who doesn't find her way into one of those magic circles of friendship will have a very difficult time trying to do research that will have an impact on the scientific world.

One of the ways a graduate student gets into these circles is by winning a teaching assistantship with an important professor. Recently, political scientist Frank Morris published a paper pointing out that African Americans are seldom awarded these assistantships. Instead, they tend to receive fellowships, which provide money but no connection with the university's research projects. Howard Adams, who runs the Graduate Engineering Degrees for Minorities program, agrees. "A fellowship is the kiss of death," he says, "because it doesn't come with anything." It doesn't lead to a relationship with a faculty mentor, and that is almost a necessity in science.

By the early 1980s, black women had gained parity with black men in the sciences, earning 50 percent of all doctorates awarded to black Americans. Still, in 1992, black Americans, who make up 12.1 percent of the population, filled only 1.9 percent of all science and engineering positions.

By and large, black women scientists in the United States have succeeded in spite of numerous barriers and in the face of tremendous odds. Most black women scientists have never had other black women as study companions, colleagues, or mentors. Indeed, many have had the experience of being the lone black female in their respective fields. Those who succeed do so by overcoming their isolation and managing to adapt to the difficult working environments they often encounter.

INTO THE FUTURE

Success in science and medicine requires hard work, long hours, and a commitment to the pursuit of knowledge for knowledge's sake. The training is long and tremendously difficult. For much of this century, successful male scientists have been afforded the opportunity to pursue their scientific interests with few interruptions. Only in the last decade of the twentieth century have black women come close to having equal access to such opportunities. Having demonstrated their commitment to the highest ideals of science, black women scientists will no doubt make greater tangible achievements in the future.

However, for that to happen, a change of attitude and opportunity must begin at the very earliest stages of education. Indeed, the change must begin with our approach to children even before they enter school. Not every child is capable of becoming a nuclear physicist or neurosurgeon. But every *kind* of child certainly is. It has taken the human race centuries to learn this simple fact, but it is one that must be made clear to every four-year-old in our country if we are not to continue to waste valuable human resources.

We have long been taught that science goes beyond superstition and preconceived ideas to the truth behind them. Science, historically, has been seen as the enemy of prejudice. Today, it is clear that prejudice against large portions of humanity has been the enemy of science, an enemy it must overcome.

A

Adams-Ender, Clara Leach
(1939–   )

Her 1987 appointment as chief of the Army Nurse Corps and director of personnel clearly indicated that Brigadier General Clara Adams-Ender, a sharecropper's daughter, had gone from "rags to respect." While not the first black woman to hold the highest position in the more than 40,000-member nurse corps (**Hazel Johnson** was first), Adams-Ender was a pacesetter in her own right.

In 1967, she became the first female in the army to qualify for and be awarded the Expert Field Medical Badge. Less than ten years later she became the first woman to be awarded the Master of Military Art and Science degree from the Command and General Staff College at Ft. Leavenworth, Kansas, in 1976. Four years later, she was selected as the first female to serve as senior marcher for 700 soldiers in the four-day, 100-mile Nijmegen March in Nijmegen, Holland. In 1982, she became the first black Army Nurse Corps officer to graduate from the U.S. Army War College. In 1984, she was named chief of the Department of Nursing at Walter Reed Army Medical Center, making her the first black nurse to hold that position.

Clara Adams was born July 11, 1939, and grew up in Wake County, North Carolina, with her five sisters and four brothers. She entered the Army Student Nurse Program during her third year of studies at North Carolina A & T State University in 1959. She married her husband, German-born Heinz Ender, in 1981.

In addition to her many firsts, Adams-Ender has served the military in the United States, Europe, and Korea and has held academic appointments in the nursing schools at the University of Maryland, Georgetown University, and Oakland University. She has also served as a member of the Defense Advisory Committee on Women in the Services and as a consultant for a children's television workshop in New York City.

An avid reader and physical fitness enthusiast, Adams-Ender is also an accomplished writer. Articles she has authored or coauthored have appeared in *Perspectives on Nursing, Today's O.R. Nurse, Medical Bulletin,* and *Nursing Management.* She is a contributor to *Ethical Decision-Making in Nursing Administration,* ed. Mary Cipriano Silva (1990).

Fluent in German, Adams-Ender is one of the most sought-after military speakers in the country. Her résumé indicates that she gave fifty-four professional presentations in 1990 alone. Yet she also found time for the community, her personal interests, her stepson, and her husband, who is a retired orthodontist and oral surgeon. She has a life membership in the **National Association for the Advancement of Colored People,** is a Red Cross nurse, and has served on the board of the Northeast

Illinois Council of the Boy Scouts of America. She was recently inducted into **Delta Sigma Theta Sorority** as an honorary member and is also a member of the **National Council of Negro Women** and the National Association for Female Executives.

Adams-Ender is a tireless worker whose many awards and honors include the military's Distinguished Service Award and Meritorious Service Medal with three oak leaf clusters; Roy Wilkins Meritorious Service Award of the NAACP; Female Athlete of the Year; Regents' Distinguished Graduate Award of the University of Minnesota; Outstanding Young Woman of America; and a place on *Washingtonian* magazine's 1989 list of the 100 most powerful women in Washington, D.C.

She is now retired from the army and is the president/CEO of CAPE (Caring About People with Enthusiasm).

LINDA ROCHELLE LANE

Alexander, Virginia M. (1900–1949)

Virginia M. Alexander, physician, was born in Philadelphia in 1900. She was one of four children. Her mother died when Alexander was four years old, and her father lost his once-successful livery stable when she was thirteen.

Despite financial burdens, Alexander and her siblings managed to continue their educations. Both she and her oldest brother, Raymond, received scholarships to the University of Pennsylvania. Raymond completed his studies at Harvard Law School and went on to become one of the most influential black lawyers in Philadelphia. To support herself in college, Virginia worked as a waitress, maid, and

clerk. A philanthropic friend of the family provided financial assistance so that she could attend the Woman's Medical College of Pennsylvania.

At Woman's Medical College, Alexander had to endure attempts by teaching staff to discourage black medical students. She persevered, however, and during her first year ranked second highest among medical aptitude test examinees. For a time following her graduation from medical school in 1925, she had trouble obtaining an internship because of her race and gender. After many refusals she was reluctantly accepted at Kansas City (Missouri) General Hospital, becoming the first female member of the hospital staff.

In 1928, Alexander returned to North Philadelphia to set up a general practice. She became increasingly concerned with the poor health care provided to women and children in black neighborhoods. In 1931, she established the Aspiranto Health Home in her own three-story dwelling to provide health care facilities and instruction to pregnant women and their children.

Following a severe illness that temporarily forced her to discontinue her practice, Alexander renewed her interest in public health matters. During the summer of 1936, she toured several European countries to observe health care techniques and practices. With this new knowledge, she felt she needed additional education to carry out her goal in the United States. In 1937, she received a master's degree in public health from Yale University.

Alexander worked in the public health field for nearly nine years, first in Washington, D.C., as a member of the U.S. Department of Health and as a staff physician at **Howard University** Medical School, and later at Schlossfield Hospital in Birmingham, Alabama. In 1941, she returned to private practice in Philadelphia. She also was on the courtesy staff of the Woman's Medical College of Pennsylvania. She continued to practice medicine until her death from lupus in 1949 at the age of forty-nine.

BRENDA GALLOWAY-WRIGHT

Anderson, Caroline (1848–1919)

One of Philadelphia's celebrated nineteenth-century black women physicians, Caroline Virginia Anderson was born in that city on November 1, 1848. Her parents, Letitia and William Still, were founders of the Underground Railroad in antebellum Philadelphia.

Anderson completed her primary and secondary education at Mrs. Henry Gordon's Private School, the Friends Raspberry Allen School, and the **Institute for Colored Youth** (now Cheyney University). In 1865, she entered **Oberlin College.** She graduated from the literary course in 1868, the youngest graduate and only black woman in a class of forty-five. During commencement ceremonies she was asked to preside over the college's Ladies Literary Society, an honor never before presented to one of her race.

After graduation, Anderson returned to Philadelphia to teach school. On December 28, 1869, at her parents' home, Anderson married former slave Edward A. Wiley, whom she had met at Oberlin. The wedding made headlines, and was attended by Lucretia Mott, Dilwyn Parrish, Robert Purvis, and many other prominent figures in the abolitionist movement.

Following the untimely death of her husband in 1873, Anderson accepted a post at

A graduate of the Women's Medical College, Caroline V. Still Anderson was one of Philadelphia's celebrated nineteenth-century black women physicians. (SCHOMBURG CENTER)

Howard University in Washington, D.C., where she taught elocution and drawing classes. While still teaching, she matriculated at Howard Medical School in 1875. The next year she transferred to the Woman's Medical College in Philadelphia, from which she graduated in March 1878. The other black woman in her class was Georgiana E. Patterson Young from New York.

On August 17, 1880, she married Matthew Anderson of Green Castle, Pennsylvania. A prominent minister and educator, he received a B.A. from Oberlin in 1874 and a doctor of divinity degree from Lincoln University in Philadelphia. Together, the Andersons helped to found the Berean Manual Training and Industrial School in 1889. The school provided training in many industrial fields as well as instruction in the liberal arts. Anderson was assistant principal of the school for thirty-two years.

Anderson also took an active interest in the concerns of the Philadelphia community. She was appointed treasurer of the Woman's Medical College Alumnae Association in 1888; was a board member of the Home for the Aged and Infirmed Colored People of Philadelphia; was president of the Berean Women's Christian Temperance Union; and helped to organize black Young Men's Christian Associations (YMCAs) in Philadelphia.

Anderson died in her Philadelphia home on June 1, 1919.

BRENDA GALLOWAY-WRIGHT

B

Bailey, Margaret E. (19??–)

Margaret Bailey was born in Selma, Alabama. She graduated from Dunbar High School in Mobile, then went on to the Fraternal Hospital School of Nursing in Montgomery and to San Francisco State College. In 1944, she entered the United States Army. After serving in a wide variety of assignments all over the United States and on a number of bases overseas, she attended a course in psychiatric nursing at Fort Sam Houston, Texas. She added that specialty to her repertoire, which already included medical and surgical nursing.

At Fitzsimmons General Hospital in Denver, Colorado, Bailey took charge of the Nightingale program, named for nursing pioneer Florence Nightingale. In this program, she recruited nurses for the army by speaking at nursing schools and meetings of local medical organizations, as well as making television appearances.

In 1964, Bailey reached the rank of lieutenant colonel. She was the first African-American nurse in the Army to do so. In 1970, she became the first African American to hold the rank of full colonel in the Army Nurse Corps.

KATHLEEN THOMPSON

Banks, Anna De Costa (1869–1930)

By any standard, Anna De Costa Banks was an exceptional nurse. Banks was born (September 2, 1869), raised, and educated in Charleston, S.C. She attended Hampton Institute in Virginia, graduating in the first class at Dixie Hospital School of Nursing at Hampton in 1891. Returning to Charleston, she became head nurse of the Hospital and School for Nurses when it opened in 1896. Committed to meeting the health care needs of the black community, these institutions were also created in response to the denial of staff privileges to black physicians and the exclusion of black women from admission to the City Hospital Training School.

From 1903 to 1930, Banks worked for the Ladies Benevolent Society (LBS) as a visiting nurse, caring for the sick poor in their homes. The white ladies of Charleston had hired Banks with some reluctance because she was black, but they quickly came to appreciate her skill, tender-heartedness, and tact. Banks knew the ill feelings that existed in Charleston between poor whites and blacks, and she entered the new field of visiting nursing with some apprehension.

She worked among people of both races, but initially her patients were what she described as the poor and ignorant class of white people. Even though the LBS had for at least seventy-five years cared for black patients, they had done so in a very carefully controlled fashion. Caring for an average of 250 patients annually, Banks cautiously constructed opportunities that allowed her to further extend LBS services to the black community. Predictably, her efforts proceeded quietly, but by 1910, the growing number of black patients and physicians served by the society documented her success.

Despite the demands of her work with the LBS, Banks remained actively involved with the Hospital and School for Nurses. The hospital's patients remained the black community's most destitute citizens, and even though supported by black churches, businessmen, and the local women's clubs, the institution was in constant financial crisis. Responding to the desperate need, Banks served as superintendent of the hospital for over twenty years without pay, in order to help keep the doors from closing. Beyond caring for the sick, she was also intent on ensuring black women's opportunities in the newly emerging profession of nursing. During her tenure she educated more than one hundred black women as nurses.

Through her work with the black hospital, training school, and the LBS, Banks quietly created an innovative matrix of care for the black community and simultaneously accustomed the white community to using black women who had been trained as nurses. She pursued her goal by supplying students as the LBS needed them. While the students provided the LBS with flexible and affordable solutions to the demands created by a fluctuating caseload, the money generated through the program provided the hospital with a dependable source of income essential for its survival.

When she died on November 29, 1930, she was honored for her untiring service to her people. Anna De Costa Banks hoped that it would be said of her that "she has done what she could"—and it was. Her alma mater claimed that no other Hampton graduate had a more vital influence upon his or her community than Anna Banks.

KAREN BUHLER-WILKERSON

Benjamin, Regina (1956–)

In the small town of Bayou La Batre, on Alabama's Gulf coast, Dr. Regina Benjamin opened a clinic. As the only doctor in this poor, rural area near the Mississippi border, Benjamin is committed to providing health care in a place few doctors care to go. More than a country doctor with a heart of gold, Dr. Benjamin is figuring out how to make rural health care work.

Born in 1956 in the city of Mobile, Benjamin was raised across the bay in the little town of Daphne, Alabama. Her mother was Millie Alphonse Benjamin, a waitress and housewife. Her father was Clarence E. Benjamin, a civil servant at a nearby air force base. Her parents separated when she was two, and by the age of nine her father was transferred to a base in California. Benjamin grew up with her mother, but remained close to both her parents.

Benjamin attended public schools and never thought about becoming a doctor. There was only one doctor in her town, and she had never even seen a black doctor. She graduated from Fair Hope High School in 1975 and went on to Xavier University, where she majored in pre-pharmacy. While in college, she was persuaded by an advisor to set her sights on becoming a doctor. She graduated from Xavier in 1979 with a degree in chemistry, and was accepted to Morehouse School of Medicine in Atlanta. After two years at Morehouse, she transferred back to the University of Alabama at Birmingham, where she received her M.D. in 1984.

Benjamin returned to Georgia for her residency, serving at the Medical Center of Central Georgia in Macon from 1984 to 1987. To help pay for her schooling, she made an agreement with the National Health Service Corps (NHSC).

Health care delivery in rural areas is a major problem in modern America. American medicine may be at the forefront of advanced technology, but those sophisticated facilities are usually found in large urban areas. There are many poor rural counties that have no doctors whatsoever, or just a few doctors to cover thousands of square miles. To lure doctors to out-of-the-way areas, the National Health Service and other organizations will pay a doctor's tuition in exchange for a few years of work in a remote area.

On completing her residency, Benjamin was assigned to a small clinic in Irvington, Alabama. Many NHSC doctors will put in their time and leave, but this was home to Benjamin. She enjoyed working with local people. After completing her work in Irvington in 1990, she opened a private practice in nearby Bayou La Batre.

Bayou La Batre is a fishing town of 2,500 people—blacks, whites, Vietnamese, and Laotians. Almost everyone makes a living from the sea, which is seasonal at best. As a result, the town is very poor. Benjamin at first told her patients to pay her when they could, then traveled long distances to moonlight in emergency rooms so as to make ends meet.

Thinking there must be a better way, she went back to get her MBA from Tulane University in New Orleans. Twice a week she traveled 250 miles round trip, until she graduated in 1991. While studying, she learned of a little-known federal law that

helps to provide funding for rural health clinics. She changed her practice to a rural health clinic, which meant that she was eligible for federal funding. It also meant that she could help more people.

Benjamin was committed not just to practicing rural medicine, but to making such medical practice possible in other places. She works with other groups and agencies, showing them how to keep a rural practice alive and running. Benjamin has served on state and national medical boards to promote rural health care, to bring medicine to all the people. She has served as the Vice Chair for the Governor's Commission on Aging, the Governor's Health Care Reform Task Force, and as a board member of the State of Alabama Board of Public Health.

In 1995, Benjamin was elected to the board of the American Medical Association, the powerful national organization of American doctors. She was elected as the Young Physician Member, a new seat on the board of trustees, designed to bring the outlook of younger doctors to the board. That same year she was invited to the White House for a two-day briefing by the Office of Women's Initiatives and Outreach, a women's leadership program.

Benjamin has become a popular public speaker, accepting speaking engagements for the AMA and other organizations. She is modest, soft-spoken, and forthright, and people find her story inspirational. She tells teenagers: "Don't quit. Never quit. Be persistent. Speak your mind and do what you feel is right."

Health care reform and government funding for medicine are controversial issues in the 1990s, given funding cuts that are likely to affect millions of people. Benjamin is working to see that rural clinics and poor people are not forgotten.

Benjamin has been chosen as the "Person of the Week" by ABC News and picked as one of the "Fifty for the Future," by *Time* magazine. She has had high-paying offers in big cities, but has turned them down. What does Benjamin say about her life? "It's the best thing in the world. Patients come up, hug you, and bring you cakes and shrimp and seafood and make you fat." What do patients say about her? "I love that woman."

And she still makes house calls.

ANDRA MEDEA

Bessent, Hattie (1926–)

Hattie Bessent, administrator, psychiatric nurse, teacher, author, and researcher, is deputy executive director of the Ethnic/ Racial Minority Fellowship Programs of the American Nurses Association (ANA). These programs assist nurses in preparing for doctorates in mental health and related specialties and award fellowships for that purpose.

Hattie Bessent was born on December 26, 1926, in Jacksonville, Florida. Her mother died when Hattie was nine, so her grandmother raised her. Bessent graduated from high school in Jacksonville, Florida. After she earned a B.S. in nursing education from Florida A & M University in 1959, she returned to Jacksonville and became the first African-American nurse to head a psychiatric unit in that city. She also received an M.S. in psychiatric nursing from Indiana University in 1962 and an Ed.D. in the psychological foundations of education from the University of Florida in 1970.

Hattie Bessent is the recipient of the 1994 Lifetime Achievement Award of the Black Nurses Association.

Hattie Bessent has accomplished many firsts for herself, African Americans, and her profession. She was the first black nurse in Florida to receive a doctorate, the first black dean of the Graduate School of Nursing at Vanderbilt University, and the first black nurse in the South to be inducted into the following honorary organizations: Phi Delta Kappa, Sigma Theta Tau, and Pi Lambda Theta. She also is a member of **Delta Sigma Theta Sorority.**

In addition, in 1977 she was appointed by President Jimmy Carter to the Presidential Task Force for the Friendship Treaty with China, and to the Presidential Commission on Mental Health. She received the Distinguished Alumna Award from Florida A & M University in 1980. She also has been awarded the **Mary Mahoney** Award by the ANA.

Bessent is the recipient of the 1994 Lifetime Achievement Award of the Black Nurses Association; the 1995 Linda Richards Award of the American Nurses Association; and the 1995 Psychiatric Nurse of the Year Award of the American Psychiatric Nurses Association. In 1995, she became a Distinguished Scholar of the American Nurses Foundation.

As the only minority director on the staff of the ANA, Hattie Bessent has worked tirelessly to ensure that professionals of color, and all nurses, continue to hone their research, clinical, and practice skills. Through her own publications, research, and administrative efforts she has fostered the principles of service—"You must give of yourself in order to be worthy"—that she learned from her grandmother years ago.

CHERYL TAYLOR

Boyd-Franklin, Nancy (1950–)

One of the foremost psychologists specializing in the issues of the black family, Nancy Boyd-Franklin is a clinical psychologist, a family therapist, an author, and a teacher passing on her knowledge to a new generation of mental health workers. She is also a pioneer in innovative techniques for bettering psychological health in the black community.

Born in Harlem on June 13, 1950, Boyd-Franklin is the daughter of Regina and Rudolph Boyd. Her father was a policeman, her mother a teacher. Her mother's

family came to Harlem from Jamaica, and her father's family came there from North Carolina. Both had strong beliefs in the importance of education. Someone who got an education had a responsibility to give something back to the community in return. These beliefs influenced Boyd-Franklin as she pursued her goal of being a psychologist.

After graduating from high school, Boyd-Franklin attended Swarthmore College, where she received her bachelor of

One of the foremost psychologists specializing in the issues of the black family, Nancy Boyd-Franklin is a clinical psychologist, a family therapist, an author, a teacher, and a pioneer in innovative techniques for bettering psychological health in the black community.

science degree in 1972. She went on to study clinical psychology at Teachers College, Columbia University, earning her M.S. in 1974 and her Ph.D. in 1977.

While first and foremost a clinical psychologist and family therapist, Boyd-Franklin has always taught as well. She wears many hats because there is so much to do. She went into private practice in New York in 1978, providing family therapy, couples therapy, and group therapy with black women; later she would move her private practice to New Jersey.

By 1980, she was also teaching on the faculty of the University of Medicine and Dentistry of New Jersey, located in Newark. There Boyd-Franklin filled two roles. She was supervising psychologist at its Community Mental Health Center until 1992, and clinical associate professor in the psychiatry department. In 1992, she accepted a professorship at Rutgers University, in the Graduate School of Applied and Professional Psychology.

Boyd-Franklin has also been involved with the issue of the psychological impact of AIDS on children and families, working as consultant to the National Pediatrics HIV Resource Center in Newark and the Children's Hospital AIDS Program. She also has developed an innovative program in home-based and community-based therapy in a black neighborhood in New Jersey. The idea is to bring psychology to the clients, instead of waiting until clients come to the clinics. (There remains a certain stigma to seeking psychological services.) Boyd-Franklin wishes to show, by outreach, that psychology has much to offer the black community. She is particularly interested in measures that can prevent drug abuse or help young people through their difficult years.

Boyd-Franklin's many publications include *Black Families in Therapy: A Multisystems Approach* (1989) and *Children, Families and HIV/AIDS: Psychosocial and Therapeutic Issues,* co-edited with Gloria L. Steiner and Mary G. Boland (1995).

Boyd-Franklin has been honored with a number of awards. In 1994, she was named Distinguished Psychologist of the Year by the Association of Black Psychologists. In 1991, she was cited for her Pioneering Contribution to the Field of Family Therapy by the American Family Therapy Association. In 1974, she was named Thomas J. Watson Fellow, which allowed her to travel extensively in East and West Africa studying language and community mental health.

Boyd-Franklin points out that her work as a psychologist has helped her to meet her own goal of having a strong family life while pursuing her professional career. She is married to Dr. Andrew J. Franklin, who is also a psychologist. She is the mother of one child and three stepchildren: Deidre, Quentin, Remi, and Jay. Of her professional life, Boyd-Franklin says: "I have been doing this for twenty years and have never had a bored moment."

ANDRA MEDEA

Bozeman, Sylvia Trimble (1947–)

Dr. Sylvia Trimble Bozeman has been a dynamic leader of the national mathematical community as chairperson of the **Spelman College** Mathematics Department, member of the Board of Governors of the Mathematical Association of America (MAA), and vice president of the National Association of Mathematicians. She co-chairs the MAA Committee on Minority Participation in Mathematics, which oversees Strengthening Underrepresented Minority Mathematics Achievement.

In 1988, Dr. Bozeman received both the White House Initiative Faculty Award for Excellence in Science and Technology and the Tenneco United Negro College Fund Award for Excellence in Teaching. In 1980, she was named "Outstanding Young Woman of America." She has published in the mathematical field of functional analysis, and recently she turned to research in the area of image processing, supported by the National Aeronautics and Space Administration. Previous research was supported through grants from the Army Research Office and the National Science Foundation.

In 1968, she received a B.S. degree in mathematics from Alabama A & M University in Huntsville. She was vice president of the student government, and second in her 200-member class. In January 1970, she received an M.A. from Vanderbilt University, where she continued her graduate studies. After a year as an instructor in the Upward Bound program of Tennessee State University in Nashville and a year on leave, she joined the faculty of Spelman College, where she is now a full professor. During three years of study leave, she earned a Ph.D. degree in mathematics from Emory University, awarded in August 1980.

Sylvia Trimble was born on August 1, 1947, in Camp Hill, Alabama, to Horance E. Trimble, Sr., and Robbie Jones Trimble.

She and her husband, Robert E. Bozeman, a professor of mathematics at Morehouse College, have a daughter and a son.

PATRICIA CLARK KENSCHAFT

Brown, Dorothy Lavinia (1919–)

> Men said that a woman wasn't able to stand up to five years of training in surgery. . . . I tried to be . . . not hard, but durable. . . . I am a fighter who learned how to get along with the male ego.

Dorothy Lavinia Brown, the first black female surgeon to become a fellow of the American College of Surgeons, learned to fight for what she wanted from a very early age. Born in Troy, New York, she was placed in an orphanage at the age of five months by her mother, Edna Brown. She did not meet her father, Kevin Thomas Brown, until she was well into adulthood. The orphanage, where Brown remained until the age of twelve, was a predominantly white institution. Brown later recalled that she was one of only a handful of black children in a "sea of white faces." Even so, it was the only home she knew, and she was reasonably happy there.

Just before her thirteenth birthday, Brown's mother reentered her life for a brief period. Fearful that her daughter would be placed in service, Edna Brown took Dorothy out of the orphanage, but by that time mother and daughter were strangers. Brown ran away from home on five separate occasions, each time returning to the Troy orphanage. Finally, at the age of fifteen, determined to get a high school education, Brown ran away again and enrolled at Troy High School. She had no place to stay and no one to live with, but the principal of the school found an appropriate living situation for the determined teenager, who was placed in the custody of foster parents, Mr. and Mrs. S. W. Redmon.

With the Redmons, Dorothy found the security, support, and stability that thus far had eluded her, and they had a significant influence on her. The Redmons considered Brown to be their daughter, and they passed along to her their Christian values and outlook. It was these values, Brown professed much later, that helped her come to terms with a growing bitterness toward white society. Ultimately she found a way to forgive oppression without relinquishing her own self-esteem and dignity.

After Brown graduated from high school, the Troy Methodist Women nominated her for a scholarship to Bennett College in Greensboro, North Carolina, and in 1937, in the midst of the Great Depression, she made her first trip south. After a shaky start, she graduated second in her class from Bennett. Fortunately, it was not until many years later that she learned Bennett administrators had advised the Troy Methodist Women to persuade Brown not to return for a second year because she was "not Bennett material."

Since the age of five, when her tonsils were removed, Brown had harbored a desire to be a doctor, and when World War II made it possible for more women to gain acceptance into medical schools, she took advantage of the opportunity. She entered Meharry Medical College in 1944 and earned an M.D. four years later. After a year's internship at Harlem Hospital, Brown began a five-year residency in surgery at Meharry and Hubbard Hospital.

Her decision to pursue surgery was met with almost universal resistance. But Brown persisted to become a fellow of the American College of Surgeons and to be appointed chief of surgery at Nashville's Riverside Hospital, a position she held from 1957 until 1983.

If her achievements were limited to her success as a physician and surgeon, Brown's life would be noteworthy, but she has been a pathbreaker in other areas as well. For example, she became the first single woman in Tennessee to adopt a child, when a young, unmarried patient begged her to adopt her newborn daughter. Brown's love for children, and her desire to help a child just as the Redmons had helped her, prompted her to begin the process. In 1956, Brown legally adopted her daughter, Lola.

In 1966, Brown was approached to run for a seat in the Tennessee state legislature when it became apparent that redistricting would make it possible to elect a black candidate. When she won, Brown became the first black woman to serve in the state legislature. Initially she indicated that she probably would return to her medical practice after two years, but it soon became clear that good planning would make it possible for her to accommodate her many roles as physician, surgeon, teacher, mother, and legislator, and she began to rethink her early decision to limit herself to one term. However, following a bitter losing battle over her sponsorship of an expanded abortion rights bill, which she claimed would have saved the lives of many Tennessee women, Brown resigned her seat and returned full time to her medical practice, her teaching career, and to caring for her daughter.

Through the early 1990s, Brown remained an active teacher and physician as well as a national and international lecturer.

CHRISTINE A. LUNARDINI

Brown, Lucy Hughes (1863–1911)

Lucy Hughes Brown, founder of the Cannon Hospital and Training School for Nurses, felt strongly the need for total commitment by the individual to the nursing profession. As associate editor of the *Hospital Herald: A Journal Devoted to Hospital Work, Nurse Training, and Domestic and Public Hygiene,* Brown wrote the following in the October 1899 issue: "She who has not first considered the matter from every standpoint should not enter the field of nursing."

Lucy Hughes Brown was born in North Carolina in April 1863. She attended Scotia Seminary and graduated in 1885. After graduating from the Woman's Medical College of Pennsylvania in 1894, she returned to her home state of North Carolina, where she practiced for two years. In 1896, Brown moved to Charleston, South Carolina, where she became the first African-American woman physician in the state. Her practice was reported to have been thriving and successful.

In 1897, she was instrumental in founding the Cannon Hospital and Training School for Nurses; it later became known as the McClennan-Banks Hospital. In addition to her position as head of the nursing program at Cannon Hospital, Brown was also editor of the *Hospital Herald* and secretary of the Cannon Hospital Association.

In 1904, Brown's health was failing rapidly, and so she retired from her practice.

She died on June 26, 1911. She was survived by her husband, Reverend David Brown, and one daughter.

MARGARET JERRIDO

Brown, Mary Louise (1868–?)

Mary Louise Brown came from a family whose members were as talented and eager as she to take advantage of post–Civil War educational and career opportunities. Brown taught school while attending evening medical classes at the **Howard University** medical department and graduated from that program in 1898. In a move that was extraordinary for her time, Brown traveled to Edinburgh, Scotland, to receive postgraduate training. For more than twenty-five years she contributed her services to the black community as both a teacher and a physician.

Her father, the Reverend John Mifflin Brown, a bishop in the African Methodist Episcopal (AME) Church, had entered the Howard medical school program soon after it opened. He failed to graduate however, because of frequent reassignments to Southern cities, where he established several black colleges. Brown's three brothers completed their professional education at Howard. One brother, John Mifflin Brown, followed a career similar to her own. He studied medicine at Howard between 1877 and 1881 and then settled in Kansas to practice medicine. Another brother became a minister; the third, a teacher.

GLORIA MOLDOW

Browne, Marjorie Lee (1914–1979)

I always, always, *always* liked mathematics! . . . As far back as I can remember, I liked mathematics because it was a lonely subject. I do have plenty of friends, and I talk with them for hours at a time. But I also like to be alone, and mathematics is something I can do completely alone.

—Marjorie Lee Browne, 1979

As one of the first two black women to earn a doctorate in mathematics (the other is **Evelyn Granville**), Marjorie Lee Browne had plenty of opportunity to act, as well as think, alone. She taught at North Carolina Central University (NCCU) from 1949 to

One of the first two black women to receive doctorates in mathematics, Marjorie Lee Browne worked for thirty years to build the mathematics department at North Carolina Central University. (PATRICIA KENSCHAFT)

1979, and for twenty-five years was the only person in the department with a Ph.D. in mathematics. Under her leadership NCCU became the first predominantly black institution to be awarded a National Science Foundation grant to maintain a summer institute for secondary teachers; she directed the mathematics section of these institutes for thirteen years.

Browne was the principal writer of a successful proposal to IBM for $60,000 to fund the first electronic digital computer at NCCU for academic computing. In 1960 and 1961, she directed the installation of this computer laboratory. In 1969, she obtained the first Shell Grant, making it possible to give awards to outstanding students in her department, a program that continued for over ten years.

Marjorie Lee was born on September 9, 1914, in Memphis, Tennessee, to Mary Taylor Lee and Lawrence Johnson Lee, a railway postal clerk. Marjorie's mother died before her second birthday, and her father remarried. Her father had attended college for two years and excelled at mental arithmetic. He shared his love of mathematics with his children and kept up with them as they earned undergraduate degrees in mathematics.

After attending public schools in Memphis, Marjorie Lee was sent to LeMoyne High School, a private high school, and then attended **Howard University**. While in high school she won the Memphis city women's tennis singles championship, and in college she sang in the Howard University choir. In 1935, she graduated cum laude.

She taught for a short while at Gilbert Academy in New Orleans; then, after earning an M.S. in mathematics from the University of Michigan in 1939, she joined the faculty of Wiley College in Marshall, Texas, and began to work on her doctorate during summers in Michigan. In 1947, she became a teaching fellow at the University of Michigan, and in 1949 she earned a doctorate in mathematics.

She won a Ford Foundation fellowship to study combinatorial topology at Cambridge University in 1952–53, and that year she also traveled throughout Western Europe. During 1958–59, she was a National Science Foundation Faculty Fellow, studying numerical analysis and computing at the University of California at Los Angeles, and she traveled in Mexico. She won a similar fellowship for the 1965–66 year, when she studied differential topology at Columbia University.

In 1975, four years before her retirement, Dr. Browne was the first recipient of the W. W. Rankin Memorial Award for Excellence in Mathematics Education, given by the North Carolina Council of Teachers of Mathematics. The award states: "She pioneered in the Mathematics Section of the North Carolina Teachers Association, helping to pave the way for integrated organizations."

Marjorie Browne had a lively personal and professional life. During her final years, she used her own money to provide financial aid to many gifted young people so they could pursue their educations. She helped many students—some of whom came to her with less than adequate preparation—to pursue the study of mathematics to the completion of the Ph.D. degree. Browne died of a heart attack on October 19, 1979.

PATRICIA CLARK KENSCHAFT

Bullock, Carrie E. (d. 1961)

Carrie E. Bullock, a black nurse who graduated from Scotia Seminary Normal Department in Concord, North Carolina, is best known for her relentless work with the Chicago Visiting Nurse Association for black people.

Very little is known of Bullock's formative years. Upon completion of her nurse's training, Bullock took a job at the Provident Hospital of Chicago in June 1909. She worked at this institution for nineteen years. During this time she also served as the assistant supervisor and then supervisor of the Chicago Visiting Nurse Association. The **National Association of Colored Graduate Nurses** (NACGN) met in Chicago in 1923, due to Bullock's efforts. It was reportedly the largest and most successful meeting ever held by that organization. During this meeting, Bullock was elected vice president of the NACGN. From this position, Bullock worked tirelessly to promote the ideas of the organization. The association's official publication, the *National News Bulletin,* was published monthly, and Bullock served as its managing editor (for how long is unknown). In 1927, Bullock was elected president of the association at the Philadelphia meeting.

Bullock's role in the NACGN has marked her as an important figure in the overall evolution of black nursing organizations. As she stated at one point in her life: "I try to practice the golden rule; I believe we get out of the world what we put into it. I wish sincerely to be just to others, and I am truly humble."

FELIX ARMFIELD

C

Canady, Alexa (1950–)

One of the few women to practice neurosurgery, Alexa Canady is a member of one of the most exclusive groups in science. She has mastered one of the most difficult technologies in existence, brain surgery. At the same time, as a black woman, she has sought to practice surgery in a more holistic, human manner. As she has said: "My job is not really to cut. My job is to help people, which often includes cutting, and that's a very different focus."

Born in Lansing, Michigan, on November 7, 1950, Canady is the daughter of Clinton Canady and Elizabeth Hortense Golden Canady. Her father was a well-respected dentist in Lansing and a graduate of Meharry Medical College, a school originally founded to educate former slaves. Her mother was a graduate of Fisk University and was active in black sorority leadership. Canady credits both her mother and her grandmother with helping to inspire her.

Canady and her brother attended local public schools, where they were the only two black students. Upon graduating from high school, Canady attended the University of Michigan at Ann Arbor. She graduated with a bachelor of science degree in 1971, and went on to the University of Michigan College of Medicine. She graduated from medical school cum laude in 1975, earning a citation from the American Medical Women's Association.

Canady completed her internship from 1975 to 1976 at New Haven Hospital, attached to Yale University. After this she was accepted for her neurosurgery residency at the University of Minnesota. She was the first woman and the first African American ever to be admitted to the program. Next, Canady completed a fellowship in pediatric neurosurgery in Philadelphia, at Children's Hospital. During this same period, she was an instructor in neurosurgery at the University of Pennsylvania.

In 1982, Canady returned to Michigan, joining the staff of Henry Ford Hospital in Detroit, where she was an instructor of neurosurgery. In 1983, she became pediatric neurosurgeon at Children's Hospital of Michigan, where she became the head of the department. She was named Teacher of the Year at Children's Hospital in 1984. This same year she became certified by the American Board of Neurological Surgery. In 1987, she became chief of neurosurgery at Children's Hospital, a position she retained along with her other duties at Henry Ford Hospital.

Canady joined the Wayne State University School of Medicine in 1985 as a clinical instructor. By 1991, she was vice chairman of the department of neurosurgery. Canady has been elected to the Michigan Woman's Hall of Fame.

Canady has excelled in science, and she readily acknowledges the black pioneers who have gone before her. "As one of the first of the new generation of black women neurosurgeons," she says, "I have a responsibility to seize hold of the opportunities created by the movement of the sixties as well as the generation before. Those of us in small, highly specialized fields have an opportunity to reaffirm the equality of black people in the entire gamut of study."

ANDRA MEDEA

Carnegie, Mary Elizabeth (1916–)

Mary Elizabeth Lancaster did not grow up with dreams of becoming a nurse. Her career came about more by chance than by choice; yet she has made a lasting mark on the profession of nursing and the history of black women in it.

Born on April 19, 1916, in Baltimore, Maryland, Mary Elizabeth Lancaster was the daughter of Adeline Beatrice Swann and John Oliver Lancaster. After her parents were divorced, Mary Elizabeth lived most of the time with her aunt and uncle in Washington, D.C., because her mother was unable to care for her. While still quite young, she began working after school and on weekends at a whites-only cafeteria, the Allies Inn.

After graduating from Dunbar High School, Lancaster left Washington for New York. Ready and willing for either work or further education, she found opportunity for neither. Then a cousin suggested that she try nursing. Lancaster applied to Lincoln Hospital School for Nurses and then returned to Washington and the steam table at the Allies Inn. In July 1934, Lancaster received a letter notifying her that she had been accepted to Lincoln.

During her training Lancaster discovered

A leader in the fight to gain professional acceptance and equality for black professional nurses, Mary Elizabeth Carnegie was the first black to be elected to the board of a state nurses' association.

that she genuinely enjoyed her work and that she had a flair for it as well. She also developed an interest in organizing and activism. She was chosen to serve as a hostess at the 1936 convention of the **National Association of Colored Graduate Nurses,** an event which encouraged Lancaster's growing interest in the fight to gain professional acceptance and equality for black professional nurses.

After Lincoln, Lancaster went to West Virginia State College, where she received a B.A. in sociology in 1942. In 1943, while assistant director of nursing at Hampton University, she established the first black baccalaureate program in nursing in Virginia. In December of 1944, she married Eric Carnegie. They divorced in 1954. In 1945, she became the first dean of the school of nursing at Florida A & M University in Tallahassee. She also became active in the battle that black professional nurses were waging to become members of the Florida State Nurses Association. Eventually, she became the first black American to be elected to the board of that or any other state association.

Over the years, Mary Elizabeth Carnegie earned a number of other degrees and awards, including a doctorate in public administration from New York University in 1972. From the early 1950s on, she held editorial positions on a number of nursing journals, traveled extensively as a consultant, and in 1986 published the book *The Path We Tread: Blacks in Nursing 1854–1984*. A second edition of the book, published in 1991, extends the coverage to 1990.

MARIE MOSLEY

Chinn, May Edward (1896–1980)

May Edward Chinn, physician, was born in Great Barrington, Massachusetts, in 1896, the only child of William Lafayette Chinn, a slave who had escaped to freedom at the age of eleven from the Chinn (Cheyne) plantation in Virginia, and his wife, who had been born on a Chickahominy Indian reservation near Norfolk, Virginia.

When May was three years old, her family moved to New York. Her mother, wishing to protect her from the distress caused by her father's alcoholism and determined that her daughter should receive a good

In 1928, physician May Edward Chinn (seated, right) joined with other black doctors to practice in the Edgecombe Sanitarium as an alternative to the predominately white and white-oriented New York hospital system. In the 1970s, after her retirement from the Strang Clinic at the age of eighty-one, the inexhaustible Chinn continued to work in three day-care centers in Harlem. (MOORLAND-SPINGARN)

education, sent her, at the age of five or six, to boarding school at the Bordentown Manual Training and Industrial School. Forced to leave school when she developed osteomyelitis, May went to live with her mother on the Tarrytown estate of the Tiffanys, a wealthy white family. Though her mother was working for the family, Chinn recalls having been raised as one of the Tiffany children: dining with them, studying the classics with them, and attending concerts with them as would any child in the house.

It was through her exposure to music while living on the Tiffany estate that Chinn's musical gifts were first nurtured. When she and her mother returned to New York after the Tiffany estate had been sold, Chinn attended grammar school and took piano lessons. When she dropped out of high school, she gave piano lessons to kindergarten children. Eventually, with encouragement from her mother, Chinn took and passed a high school equivalency exam. She entered Teachers College, Columbia University, in 1917. After her first year, she changed her major from music to science and graduated in 1921. While still in college, she played and sang in concerts around New York, accompanying such celebrated performers as Paul Robeson and singing for soldiers under the auspices of the United Service Organizations.

In 1926, Chinn became the first Negro (the designation that she preferred) woman to obtain a medical degree from Bellevue Hospital Medical College. She went on to become the first Negro woman to hold an internship at Harlem Hospital, and the first woman physician to ride with the ambulance crew of the Harlem Hospital on emergency calls. In 1928, she joined the

ranks of a group of black doctors who practiced in the Edgecombe Sanitarium, an alternative establishment to the predominantly white New York hospital system. She received a master's degree in public health from Columbia University in 1933.

Well known by the end of her career for her work with regard to the early detection and diagnosis of cancer, she was on staff at the Strang Clinic until her retirement at the age of eighty-one, after which she continued her work in three day-care centers in Harlem. She was a member of the U.S. Surgeon General's advisory commission on urban affairs, and she received an honorary doctor of science degree from Columbia University in 1980.

SUSAN SHIFRIN

Clark, Mamie Phipps (1917–1983)

She did what most other scientists only get to dream about. She used science and research not only to change people's lives, but to change her country. Mamie Phipps Clark took her interest in childhood development and combined it with keen scientific ability to research the effects of segregation. This resulted in data that was used to help overturn school segregation in the United States.

Clark was born Mamie Phipps on October 18, 1917, in Hot Springs, Arkansas. Even though she came of age in the Depression, her parents were determined to send their children to college. In 1934, it was rare for Southern blacks to enter Ivy League colleges and impossible to enter the larger Southern universities. Clark won a merit scholarship to **Howard University**, the school of choice for black Southerners at the time.

The research on the socialization of black children done by Mamie Phipps Clark and her husband, Kenneth Clark, was instrumental evidence in the Brown v. Board of Education *Supreme Court decision, which outlawed separate educational facilities for the races.*

Howard boasted a remarkable teaching staff. Because segregation kept most black intellectuals out of mainstream academia, there was an extraordinarily rich talent pool at the black schools. At Howard, Ralph Bunche taught political science, Alain Locke taught philosophy, and Francis C. Sumner taught psychology.

Clark studied among these great minds at Howard from 1934 until 1938. She originally wanted to become a math teacher but, because of the condescending attitude of math teachers towards women, Clark began to explore other fields. Kenneth Clark, her future husband and research partner, encouraged her to study psychology. She excelled, and was encouraged by the staff.

Even though there were no black women teaching in the psychology department at Howard—and no black women with advanced degrees in the program—Clark continued her studies. After graduating with a bachelor of science degree in 1938, she found a job as a secretary in the law office of William Houston. This was the center of legal activity challenging segregation, even at this early date. There, Clark began her association with Thurgood Marshall, the future Supreme Court justice.

Clark continued her education at Howard in pursuit of a master's degree in psychology, having by then married Kenneth Clark. (The couple had two children: a daughter, Kate, and a son, Hilton.) Her husband suggested that she go to New York, where Ruth and Gene Horowitz (later Ruth and Gene Hartley) were doing developmental studies on self-identification with preschool children. They suggested that more such work needed to be done with black children. Clark conducted research on the subject for her master's thesis, entitled, "The Development of Consciousness of Self in Negro Pre-School Children." She was awarded a master's degree in 1939.

Clark brought up the question of how black children acquire and respond to a sense of racial identity. That is, how and when do they realize they are black? And what does it mean to them? Her husband joined her in this work, and over the years they jointly published a series of articles on black children. They were awarded a Rosenwald Fellowship for this work in

1940, the fellowship being renewed for the next two years. This made it possible for Clark not only to continue her research but to enroll for her Ph.D. at Columbia University.

Columbia University was another of the centers for psychology in that era. Clark was the only black person there, student or faculty. Her husband had earned his Ph.D. at Columbia the year before she began, the first black student to do so. Clark became the second. No other African American was to receive a Ph.D. in psychology at Columbia over the next forty years.

Prejudice was intense. Clark's sponsoring professor, Dr. Henry E. Garrett, assumed she was getting her Ph.D. so she could return to the South and teach schoolchildren. Years later, as Clark became an expert on desegregation, she and Garrett were opposing psychologists testifying in a school desegregation case. She never saw her old professor and sponsor again.

Clark earned her Ph.D. in psychology from Columbia in 1943. During the 1940s, she and her husband published a series of articles on their research with schoolchildren. Their research established that black children realize that they are black around the age of three and, with that realization, gain a negative self-identity because of prejudice. This research was cited in a series of school desegregation cases in South Carolina, Delaware, and Virginia.

In 1953, the NAACP was preparing to challenge school segregation throughout the United States in a case before the Supreme Court. Clark's research became instrumental in that effort. In the 1954 *Brown* v. *Board of Education* decision, the Supreme Court voted to overturn school segregation, citing documentation from the Clarks' studies.

Finding a job was not easy for a black female psychologist in the 1940s. At one point, Clark had to watch as less qualified white candidates took high-paying jobs at a broadcasting network. In later years she found considerable satisfaction in being named to the board of trustees of the ABC television network.

Finally, in 1944, Clark secured a job analyzing data on nurses throughout the country. She was over-qualified but, since there were no other jobs, she stayed on for a year for the research experience. Next, she found work as a research psychologist with the armed services, staying there from 1945 to 1946. While this was a somewhat better situation, she still did not feel she was doing the kind of work she was qualified to do.

At about this time, Clark began to perform psychological tests at the Riverdale Home for Children, a shelter for homeless black girls. At this time she began to realize how serious the lack of psychological services for minorities was, even in a major city like New York. Clark and her husband tried to persuade private agencies in Harlem to begin offering psychological services, but prejudice against psychology was strong. They were told either that psychological services were not needed or that they were not relevant to black children. Clark and her husband decided to open their own agency and offer the services themselves.

With the help of friends who donated their professional services, they opened the Northside Center for Child Development in 1946. Clark became its executive director. It was the first full-time child guidance center in Harlem offering psychological services. At first people did not accept it. No one wanted their children to be stigmatized as "crazy." The breakthrough in acceptance came when children in the school system were classified as "mentally retarded." Parents wanted their children reevaluated, and the center proved that many of these children were being wrongly diagnosed. With intervention from the center, most of these children were returned to mainstream classes.

At this point, Clark began to recognize the importance of education in psychological work. The center added remedial mathematics and reading to their program for children. They were the first psychological center to conceive of education as an essential component of mental health, and to provide instruction as part of their service.

The Northside Center led the way in defining new approaches for working with black children. The Clarks recognized that the psychological problems faced by minority children were not "all in their heads," but largely caused by segregation and the pressures of ghetto life. Mainstream psychology was not prepared to cope with this; Clark and her team were. They extended psychological care to political advocacy. They felt there was little point in helping people to get better if they were to continue to live under the same appalling conditions. Among other things, the Northside Center began to successfully lobby for decent housing.

Clark was also extremely active in community and business affairs. She was the chairman of the housing company that built Schomburg Towers at 110th Street and Central Park East in New York City, and she served on the boards of the American Broadcasting Companies, the Museum of Modern Art, the New York Public Library, and Teachers College at Columbia University.

Clark felt strongly that psychologists needed to *prevent* mental disturbance, not just treat it. In order to do that, society as a whole needed to be put in balance. Her work helped to put in place many basic rights that we take for granted today.

Clark died of cancer at her home in Hastings-on-Hudson, New York, on August 11, 1983.

ANDRA MEDEA

Cole, Rebecca J. (1846–1922)

Rebecca J. Cole was born on March 16, 1846, in Philadelphia, Pennsylvania. She was the second black woman physician and the first black woman to graduate from the Woman's Medical College of Pennsylvania.

Cole completed her secondary education in Philadelphia at the **Institute for Colored Youth** (ICY), now Cheyney University. While at ICY, she received a $10 prize for "excellence in classics and mathematics, and for diligence in study, punctuality of attendance, and good conduct." She graduated from ICY in 1863.

Cole received her medical degree from the Woman's Medical College in 1867. Eventually she moved to New York, where she was appointed resident physician at the New York Infirmary for Women and Children, a hospital entirely owned and operated by women physicians. Elizabeth Blackwell, the first American woman physician to receive a medical degree, described Cole as an intelligent young black physician who performed her duties with tact and care. Impressed by Cole's work, Blackwell assigned her to the post of sanitary visitor, a position in which she visited families in slum neighborhoods and instructed them in family hygiene and in infant and prenatal care.

After practicing medicine in Columbia, South Carolina, for a short time, Cole returned to Philadelphia and opened an office in the South Philadelphia section of the city. In 1873, with the assistance of fellow physician Charlotte Abbey, Cole founded a Women's Directory Center to provide medical and legal services to destitute women and children.

Cole practiced medicine for fifty years. She died in Philadelphia on August 14, 1922.

BRENDA GALLOWAY-WRIGHT

Cowings, Patricia (1948–)

Humans have adapted to many environments, but we have yet to adapt to space. Patricia Cowings is a scientist who is a leader in the uses of biofeedback to help humans adjust to weightlessness (microgravity) and motion sickness. Her techniques train people to use their minds to control their bodies' reactions, rather than relying on drugs to solve the problem.

Cowings was born on December 15, 1948, in New York City, and grew up in the Bronx. Her father, Albert S. Cowings, owned and ran a grocery store. Her mother, Sadie S. Cowings, went back to school at the age of fifty-five and became a teacher with the New York City public schools. Cowings' three siblings were all males. One of her brothers became a two-star general. With five uncles as well, she felt she had to work hard in order to prove herself.

Cowings attended Music and Art High School in the Bronx. She became interested in space at the age of eleven, but she had other interests as well. After graduating from high school, she went to the State University of New York at Stony Brook because she was interested in psychology and Stony Brook had an outstanding program. For the next four years she majored in psychology and worked as a research assistant. In 1970, she graduated with honors.

Cowings then went on to graduate studies in psychology at the University of California (UC) at Davis. While in graduate school, Cowings continued to work on research projects in addition to being a teaching assistant. While at UC she encountered Neal E. Miller, the creator of a new field that later became known as biofeedback. Biofeedback techniques train people to control voluntarily aspects of their bodies such as breathing, heartbeat and blood pressure. Cowings became fascinated by this work.

Meanwhile, she was also intrigued by engineering and her old interest in space. She joined an engineering class in which she was involved in designing a spacecraft that would help to protect astronauts from motion sickness. Motion sickness is more than just an inconvenience to space travelers. It seriously affects their ability to function in space during short or long flights, as well as while working in manned space stations.

Cowings first began to work with NASA in 1971, while still a graduate student in a summer program at the Ames Research Center. She completed both her master's in psychology and her doctorate in psychology/neurophysiology in 1973.

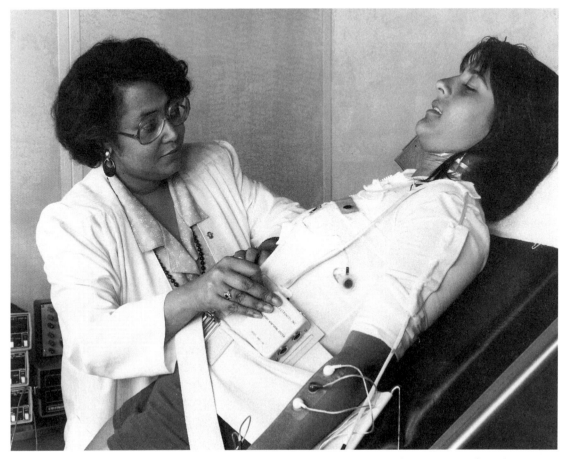

Patricia Cowings jokes that her job is to make people sick—so that she can train them how to get better. She has designed the training program and the equipment to teach astronauts how to keep their bodies functioning in zero gravity. She is a leader in the uses of biofeedback to help humans adjust to weightlessness and motion sickness. (NASA)

Upon completing her doctorate, Cowings was awarded a postdoctoral associateship by the National Research Council. This meant she could spend the next two years working at the Ames Research Center, expanding her work on preventing motion sickness in astronauts. During this period, Cowings became the first American woman to receive scientist-astronaut training, provided to her so that she would have a better understanding of the conditions

the astronauts faced. She became principal investigator in a project exploring biofeedback for uses in space.

By 1976, Cowings had begun to publish her findings on the uses of biofeedback to prevent motion sickness and other human problems. Biofeedback was important for a great many reasons. For instance, drugs can solve some of the problems of motion sickness, but they may also create unwanted side effects that can affect performance. Cowings published a number of articles on her findings, ranging over a variety of topics.

In 1978, NASA hired Cowings to be head of the Psychophysiological Research Laboratory. Since then she has conducted several experiments both in space and on the ground. In 1979, she married her lab partner, William B. Toscano, with whom she has worked for over two decades.

While American scientists have been somewhat reluctant to explore biofeedback as a solution to some of the problems encountered in space, the Soviets have been quicker to adopt Cowings' findings. In 1980, Cowings presented her findings on the uses of biofeedback at a joint U.S./Soviet meeting held in the Soviet Union. The Russians had soon incorporated her concepts into their cosmonaut training program, while the Americans still didn't know what to make of them. In the ensuing years, Cowings also worked with the Japanese space agency on their project Spacelab J.

Because of her work with astronauts, Cowings has been the topic of several television programs on her work, including the Nova and Discover series on PBS. She has been honored with any number of awards, including the Ames Honors Award for excellence in science in 1985, and the Innovative Research Award by the Biofeedback Society of California in 1990. In 1993, Cowings was appointed professor of psychiatry at the Neuropsychiatric Institute of the UCLA medical school, although she is a psychologist.

Cowings is a charter member of the Aerospace Human Factors Association. She was elected a fellow of that organization in 1993. She was also elected an associate fellow of the Aerospace Medical Association in 1986.

While Cowings continues to serve as head of the research lab at NASA's Ames Research Center, she is also collaborating with the U.S. Army and Coast Guard on projects involving motion sickness. She gave a series of lectures on her biofeedback techniques at the Mayo Clinic in 1994. Her biofeedback research has contributed to helping patients withstand the nausea that often accompanies chemotherapy.

Cowings has eased many barriers for black women in the fields of engineering and aerospace. She has shown great courage in following her dreams and setting her own course.

ANDRA MEDEA

Crumpler, Rebecca Lee (b. 1833)

"I early conceived a liking for and sought every opportunity to be in a position to relieve the suffering of others." These are the words of the first black woman to receive a medical degree in the United States.

Born in Richmond, Virginia, in 1833, Rebecca Lee was raised in Pennsylvania by her aunt, who served as a doctor to her community. Influenced by her aunt, Lee sought every opportunity to help others. Between 1852 and 1860, she worked as a nurse in Massachusetts. Then, upon the recommendations of her employers, she entered the New England Female Medical College in Boston and in March 1864 became the first and only black woman to obtain the "doctress of medicine" degree from that school.

After graduating, Lee practiced in Boston, but at the end of the Civil War she moved her practice to Richmond, Virginia, where she worked with newly freed people. After years of running a successful practice in Richmond, she moved back to Boston and, in 1883, published *A Book of Medical Discourses in Two Parts*. Based on Crumpler's personal journals, the book offered advice to women on how to provide medical care to their children and themselves.

Rebecca Lee Crumpler is an inspiration not only because she opened the doors of the medical profession to black women but also because she devoted her life's work to the study of diseases affecting women and children.

ALLISON JOLLY

D

Darden, Christine (19??–)

Christine Darden always liked to fix things and solve problems. As a three-year-old, her mother, a schoolteacher in Union County, North Carolina, took her along to school instead of leaving her with a babysitter. Even at that young age Darden responded to the numbers and figures of math and geometry. Her father was so impressed when he saw her fixing her own bicycle that he brought her a set of tools. She loved math so much that she took every possible class when she was in high school. Unfortunately, the school didn't offer the higher-level math courses she wanted to take, and she certainly wasn't allowed into the shop class.

When Christine Darden entered Hampton Institute in Virginia, she had to balance her dreams against the sexism of the times. For black women of the era, the teaching profession offered greater opportunities than those in science and math, so Darden took higher-level mathematics courses and classes in education. She graduated in 1962 with a teaching degree. From 1962 through 1965, she taught math in high schools in Virginia. In 1966, she moved to Virginia State College, where she taught classes and pursued her own education; she earned her master's degree in mathematics in 1967.

Darden then joined the National Aeronautics and Space Administration (NASA). She developed an interest in engineering, although there was general disapproval at the time because engineering was not a "woman's profession." In 1973, she was given the classification of aerospace engineer. She received her doctorate in engineering from George Washington University in Washington D.C., in 1983.

Still at NASA but now the leader of the Sonic Boom Group at the Advanced Vehicles Division in Hampton, Virginia, Ms. Darden is working on the design of a supersonic transport. The task is to develop one without the associated sonic boom. If we ever have supersonic transports moving people from New York to Los Angeles in an hour, then we will have Christine Darden to thank.

HILARY MAC AUSTIN

Davis, Frances Elliott (1882–1965)

Frances Elliott Davis rose above much adversity to become the first black nurse to be officially recognized by the American Red Cross.

Born in 1882 in Knoxville, Tennessee, "Fannie" had a white mother and a father of mixed Cherokee and black American ancestry. Fannie's mother, Emma Elliott, was ousted from her family as a result of having given birth to her. Emma Elliott spent the last five years of her ailing life in the mountains of Tennessee and, in 1887, died of tuberculosis, leaving her five-year-old daughter to the orphanage society.

Fannie Elliott lived with numerous families throughout Tennessee, North Carolina, and Pennsylvania, and developed a desire to care for others. The last family that young Fannie Elliott stayed with were the Vickerses, a black family who took her to Pittsburgh, Pennsylvania. Mr. Vickers took Elliott in as a servant, forcing her to provide for herself financially. A wealthy jewelry store owner in Pittsburgh, Joseph Allison Reed, and his wife offered Elliott domestic employment in their home. The Reeds grew fond of Elliott and became her greatest patrons throughout her academic and professional life.

Fannie Elliott received teacher training at Knoxville College, from which she graduated in 1907, but a career in nursing was her lifelong dream.

Elliott pursued this career in 1910 by entering the Freedmen's Hospital Training School in Washington, D.C. Graduating in 1912, she then did three years of private duty work in Washington, D.C. Nurse Elliott then decided to apply to the American Red Cross. She was informed that in order to do Red Cross work she would need further training in public health or rural nursing. She completed the necessary training in one year at Columbia University and received her first call to duty with the Red Cross in July 1917 in Jackson, Tennessee.

Nurse Elliott was initially denied official recognition by the Red Cross because it had not begun to enroll "colored" nurses. A few days after the initial notice in 1919, however, she received a package that contained the Red Cross nurse's pin. Inscribed on the back of the pin was 1A. The "A" indicated that she was a "colored" nurse. It was not until after World War II that the Red Cross discontinued this practice.

Fannie Elliott Davis thereafter spent her life as a public-and private-duty nurse, organizing at Detroit's Dunbar Hospital the first training school in the state of Michigan for black nurses, and later working for the Detroit Nurses Association and the Detroit Department of Health. She devoted her private life to her husband William A. Davis (whom she married on December 24, 1921) and a host of friends and relatives. Nurse Davis never lived to receive the recognition that would be given her by the American Red Cross in 1965. Fannie Elliott Davis died shortly before, in May of that year, in Mount Clemens, Michigan.

She had belonged to numerous organizations, including the Freedmen's Hospital Alumnae Association, the **National Association of Colored Graduate Nurses,** the American Red Cross, the National Organization for Public Health Nursing, the League of Nursing Education, the Detroit District and Michigan State Nurses Association, and the American Nurses Association.

FELIX ARMFIELD

Dickens, Helen Octavia (1909–)

Helen Octavia Dickens is a proud and imposing figure among the ranks of African-American women physicians.

She was born to Charles and Daisy Jane Dickens on February 21, 1909, in Dayton, Ohio. Her father was a former slave who had legally changed his name after meeting the writer Charles Dickens.

As a child, after seeing a visiting nurse and watching a physician who came into her home to care for family members, Helen decided to become a physician. Helen's father died when she was eight years old, and it was her mother who prodded, encouraged, and supported her educational efforts. After graduating from high school, Helen lived with her mother's aunt, a college-educated woman who also encouraged her. She graduated from Roosevelt High School and then attended Crane Junior College, Chicago, Illinois. She went on to graduate from the University of Illinois with an M.D. in 1933.

Helen Dickens married Purvis Sinclair Henderson, a pediatric neurosurgeon, in 1943. They had two children: Jayne and Norman Sinclair. Her husband died early in their marriage, and she raised the children with the help of her mother, who came to live with her, and a long-time female friend who became a live-in helper.

Dickens and her husband had settled in Philadelphia, where she established an obstetrics and gynecology practice. She worked extensively on the issues of teenage pregnancy prevention, the necessity of Pap smears, and the recruitment of minority students into the health care field. During her practicing years, she was affiliated with Mercy Douglass Hospital (now defunct), the Medical College of Pennsylvania, and the University of Pennsylvania, where she was the associate dean of minority affairs and a professor of obstetrics and gynecology.

As a doctor with an obstetrics and gynecology practice, Helen Octavia Dickens worked extensively on the issues of teenage pregnancy prevention, the necessity of Pap smears, and the recruitment of minority students into the health care field. (MEDICAL COLLEGE OF PENNSYLVANIA)

In her long career, many awards and honors have been bestowed upon her, including the Gimbel Award, the Distinguished Daughters of Pennsylvania Award, and admittance as a Fellow of the American College of Surgeons. She is a member of the American Medical Association, American Medical Women's Association, **The Links, Inc.**, and the **Delta Sigma Theta Sorority.**

MARGARET JERRIDO

E

Edwards, Lena Frances (1900–1986)

In 1964, President Lyndon Baines Johnson awarded Lena Frances Edwards, M.D., the Presidential Medal of Freedom, the highest award for service granted to a civilian. No other obstetrician-gynecologist has ever received this honor. Given Lena Frances Edwards' dedication to her profession and devotion to providing medical services to migrant workers and other low-income women, it is understandable that she was singled out.

Lena Edwards was born in Washington, D.C., on September 17, 1900, to Marie Coakley Edwards and Thomas Edwards. She was the valedictorian of her 1917 Dunbar High School class. She began her career in community practice in 1924 upon graduation from **Howard University** College of Medicine. Skillful attendance at home deliveries established her reputation in obstetrics.

In 1931, Edwards was appointed to the first medical staff of the Margaret Hague Maternity Hospital in Jersey City, New Jersey. She served as assistant gynecologist until 1945, when the color and gender bars were lifted and she was allowed an opportunity for specialized training. Late in life she revealed that it had been the departmental secretary who had exposed the availability of positions and embarrassed the chairman into accepting her. In 1948, she passed the oral examination of the American Board of Obstetrics and Gynecology.

Dr. Edwards' biography recounts that she was rebuffed by the medical establishment upon return to her still-segregated hometown of Washington, D.C. However, by the time she was forty-eight, she had become one of the first African-American women to be certified in her specialty. For three decades, in part because of Edwards, the Hague Hospital was among the leading clinical centers in the country, renowned for research on the hypertensive conditions of pregnancy. Indeed, the first issue of volume one of the hospital's *Bulletin* contains a description of a patient under Dr. Edwards' care.

In 1954, after many years at the Hague Hospital, Dr. Edwards returned to Howard University as a faculty member. Then, in 1959, she redefined her course in midlife. A devout Roman Catholic, she subsidized the founding of Our Lady of Guadeloupe Maternity Clinic in Hereford, Texas. She provided medical services for migrant workers at the clinic. It was this work for which President Johnson awarded her the Presidential Medal of Freedom.

Dr. Edwards returned to New Jersey in 1965. Her efforts to introduce Pap smear screening to low-income women were recognized in 1973 by an award presented by Dr. LaSalle D. Lefall, the cancer surgeon who became the first African-

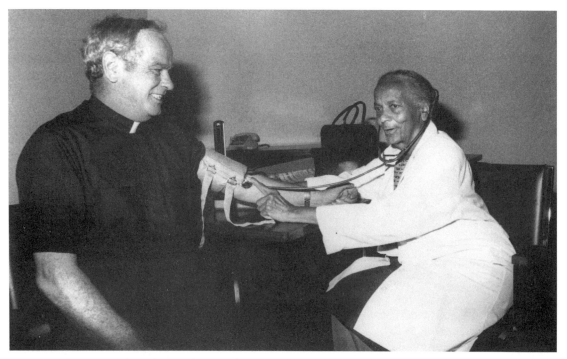

Dr. Lena Frances Edwards was honored as a "Living Legend" by Howard University's medical alumni in 1984. For her dedication to the medical profession and her devotion to providing medical services to migrant workers and other low-income women, she received the Presidential Medal of Freedom in 1964.

American president of the American Cancer Society.

Dr. Edwards endowed a scholarship fund at Howard University for students interested in family medicine. In 1984, the medical alumni association honored her as a "Living Legend." She received honorary doctorates from St. Peter's College in Jersey City and the University of Portland.

Lena Edwards died on December 3, 1986. She had married a medical school classmate, Dr. Keith Madison, and they had six children. Of these, Edward Madison and Marie Madison Metoyer are practicing physicians. She also was survived by sons Paul, John, and Thomas, and daughter Genevieve, sixteen grandchildren, and six great-grandchildren.

DEBORAH SMITH

Elders, Joycelyn Jones (1933–)

"If we think education is expensive, try ignorance. And we've tried ignorance a very long time. We've sacrificed our children." Joycelyn Elders was speaking specifically about health education when she made this striking statement, because for fifteen remarkable months, she was responsible for this nation's health as surgeon general of the United States. She was the

An advocate of changing public policy to change health, Lena Edwards is shown here pleading with the governor of Georgia (Atlanta, 9/7/76) to provide programs to allow senior citizens to remain in their own homes.

second woman and the first African American to hold that position.

Joycelyn Jones Elders was born on August 13, 1933, in Schaal, Arkansas. Her parents were sharecroppers, and her father hunted raccoons to help feed the family; he sold the skins to Sears. The family of ten lived in a three-room cabin without electricity or indoor plumbing. The children chopped cotton along with their parents from the time they were five years old. They frequently missed school during harvest time and, at other times, had to finish a share of work in the fields before leaving for school.

Elders walked five miles every school day to catch a bus that would take her to an all-black school. The trip was all of thirteen miles. And yet, in spite of the difficulties, she held out a hope of going to college. When she graduated from high

school at fifteen, she won a scholarship from the United Methodist Church that would help with tuition. But the question remained whether her family could spare their oldest child as a worker. In a *Harper's Bazaar* interview, Elders explained that "my grandmother told me, 'Minnie'—that's what I was called—'Minnie, go on and go to college' because she had enough 'young uns' with shoulders for me to stand on that I didn't have to worry."

There remained only the problem of bus fare. Elders had to get to Little Rock, where Philander Smith College was located. And so she, her parents, and all her brothers and sisters took an extra job picking cotton to raise money for her ticket. In an interview with *Ebony,* Elders said:

I don't like to talk about this very much, but it's something I have never forgotten. My young brother, he was about six at the time, had been picking cotton all day. He was so tired, but he didn't want to quit. So he just looked up at me—I can still see those great big eyes—and asked, "Do we have enough yet?" When I left, I was determined that every single one of them who wanted to go to college was going to.

With her help, five of the seven did go to college. The little brother with the big eyes is now a minister with a Ph.D.

At school, Elders became interested in medicine and science. She resolved to become a lab technician, the highest vocational goal she could imagine at the time. And then Edith Irby Jones, the first black woman to attend the University of Arkansas School of Medicine, came to speak at the campus. Elders decided immediately to follow in her footsteps.

Elders worked as a maid to pay her expenses at Philander Smith, but she still took only three years to graduate. In 1952, after her graduation, she entered the United States Army as a first lieutenant and served as a physical therapist. After her stint, she went to the University of Arkansas medical school on the G. I. Bill. She was graduated in 1960, the only black woman in her class.

However, before she graduated, she made some extra money doing high school physicals for athletes. When she arrived at a local high school, she was greeted by the tall, handsome coach. After she managed to convince him that she actually was the doctor, he asked her out. Two months later, Oliver Elders and Joycelyn Jones were married.

Elders served her internship at the University of Minnesota Hospital in Minneapolis. She then went on, in 1961, to become a resident in pediatrics at the University of Arkansas Medical Center in Little Rock. By 1963, she was chief pediatric resident. At this time, she was only thirty years old.

There could have been difficulties with a young, black woman supervising white, male doctors. However, Elders' supervisor, Dr. Panos, laid down the law to the other residents. With his support, and her own forceful personality, Elders was able to handle the situation without any significant problems. It certainly did not hurt that she was a brilliant doctor. Within a year, she was a pediatric research fellow. In 1967, she received a master's degree in biochemistry from the University of Arkansas School of Medicine and then joined the faculty. Nine years later, in 1976, she was a full professor, and two years after that, she was board-certified as a pediatric endocrinologist.

The next landmark in Elders' career came when she wrote the governor of Arkansas, Bill Clinton, a letter. It was, in her words, "a very long, very critical letter" about his policies toward health during his first term. The result was that, in 1987, he asked her to leave the university and become Arkansas' chief public health director. Everyone was very surprised, including Elders. "I said, 'Governor, when I made those recommendations, I didn't mean I was the one to implement them.'"

But Clinton thought she was, and he was right. During the time she was in office, supervising 2,600 employees, the number of early childhood medical screenings provided by the state jumped from 4,000 in 1988 to 45,000 in 1992. The immunization rate for two-year-olds rose from 34 percent to 60 percent. From 1990 to 1992, there was a 17 percent increase in the number of women participating in the state's prenatal care program. These are only a few of the dozens of improvements Elders made in health care in Arkansas.

She was better known, however, for her frank and straightforward approach. From the beginning of her time in office, she ruffled feathers with her plain speaking. At the first joint press conference she had with then-governor Clinton, she declared that she had plans for school-based health clinics, in part to deal with the rising teenage pregnancy rate. She was asked if the clinics would provide contraceptives. Her reply was, "Well, I'm not going to put them on their lunch trays, but yes." Virtually every report of the incident says that Clinton turned bright red but supported her.

Clinton's attitude seemed to be the same after he was elected president and chose

Elders as surgeon general. Her stands on birth control, abortion, and sex education made her an unpopular candidate among more conservative elements of the population. Before her confirmation in office, she was attacked on every front. She even received death threats. Nonetheless, she was confirmed.

The most obvious, and in many ways the most important, part of the surgeon general's job is to talk—about the medical needs of the nation and what to do about them. Joycelyn Elders definitely knew how to talk. She made statements that were short, to the point, and very memorable. Once, when asked about being pro-abortion, she said, "Nobody in the world is pro-abortion. . . . I'm about preventing pregnancy. I've never known a woman to need an abortion who wasn't already pregnant." When asked about sex education, she remarked that it was absurd to offer driver's education and not sex education. "We taught them what to do in the front seat of a car. Now it's time to teach them what to do in the backseat."

These and other statements kept Elders always in the center of controversy. And her opponents' habit of quoting her out of context had at least as much to do with that as her remarkable ability to turn a phrase. At one point, the media loudly announced that she had come out in favor of legalizing drugs. In fact, her exact words were "I do feel we'd markedly reduce our crime rate if drugs were legalized. I don't know all the ramifications, but I do feel we need to do some studies."

At that point, Clinton still stood behind her, whether he was comfortable doing so or not. Then, in December of 1994, Elders was again quoted out of context, this time with regard to masturbation. That taboo subject did what drugs, AIDS, and condoms could not do. Clinton demanded Elders' resignation.

Elders returned to the University of Arkansas Medical School. Some state politicians tried to block her return, but they were unsuccessful.

Joycelyn Elders had once said that she would not give up under the attacks of her opponents because she remembered that she went to Washington "to be the voice and vision for the poor and powerless." She says: "I think of all those young people out there who can't get where I can. So for all those who think I'm going to get tired and quit, they can just forget about it."

She didn't quit; one suspects she still hasn't.

KATHLEEN THOMPSON

Ellis, Effie O'Neal (1913–)

In 1970, when Effie O'Neal Ellis assumed the position of special assistant for health services to the American Medical Association (AMA), she became the first black woman physician to hold an administrative post or executive office with the AMA. That same year, the National Medical Association bestowed upon Ellis its prestigious Trailblazer Award.

Effie O'Neal Ellis was born in Harkinsville, Georgia, on June 15, 1913. She was the daughter of Joshua P. and Althea (Hamilton) O'Neal. A bright and talented student, Effie received an A.B. with honors from **Spelman College** in 1933 and a master's degree in biology from Atlanta University in 1935. In June 1935, she married Arthur W. Ellis.

During her graduate study at Atlanta University, Effie O'Neal received a grant to study diseases and parasites in Puerto Rico. During her stay, she noted the numerous health problems faced by poor people in ghettos and economically depressed rural areas, and the need for more physicians and better health care facilities. These observations convinced her to become a physician.

O'Neal was admitted to the University of Illinois College of Medicine, where she graduated, on June 16, 1950, fifth in her class. She was among twenty-three of 160 medical students to graduate with honors.

From 1950 to 1951, O'Neal served her internship at the University of Illinois Hospital, followed by her residency in pediatrics at the Massachusetts General Hospital from 1951 to 1952. She was awarded a postdoctoral fellowship to study heart trouble in children at Johns Hopkins University School of Medicine from 1952 to 1953. She also was appointed staff physician at Johns Hopkins from July 1951 to June 1953, and again from July 1956 to July 1957.

On March 23, 1953, she married James D. Solomon, a doctor from Meharry College in Tennessee who had a Ph.D. from the University of Illinois. Solomon was appointed to the staff of the Elizabeth Hospital in Washington, D.C., in 1953, where he remained until his retirement in 1983.

From 1953 to 1961, O'Neal served as director of medical education and the house pediatrician at Provident Hospital in Baltimore, Maryland. She then held a post as director of maternal and child health for the Ohio State Department of Health in Columbus, Ohio, from 1961 to 1965.

O'Neal traveled all over the United States, speaking to various medical establishments and community and educational groups. She stressed the importance of family planning and prenatal and postnatal care for families in poor communities. In order to influence policy decisions, she served in numerous capacities for the federal government, including an appointment as chairwoman for a panel at the White House conferences on food and nutrition (1969); as the first regional commissioner for social and rehabilitation services; and as regional medical director for the U.S. Department of Health, Education and Welfare Children's Bureau.

From 1970 to 1975 she served in her post as special assistant for health services to the AMA.

She is a member of the National Medical Association, the American Public Welfare Association, the American Association for Maternal and Child Health, Alpha Omega Alpha, and **Delta Sigma Theta** sororities. Among her many honors, she is an honorary fellow of the School Health Association.

Effie O'Neal Ellis currently resides in Chicago, Illinois.

BRENDA GALLOWAY-WRIGHT

Epps, Roselyn Payne (1930–)

A strong advocate for medical service for the poor, Roselyn Epps has been a practicing pediatrician, teacher, administrator, and organizational leader. The first black woman to serve as president of the American Medical Women's Association (AMWA), in 1990–91, Roselyn Payne was born in Little Rock, Arkansas, in December 1930. She matriculated at **Howard Univer-**

sity, receiving her B.S. in 1951 and her M.D. in 1955.

She served her internship and residency at Freedmen's Hospital, where she was chief resident. Later she obtained her M.P.H. from Johns Hopkins University, and her M.A. from the American University in 1981. During the 1970s, Epps served in various medical capacities in the government of the District of Columbia. Since 1981, she has been a professor of pediatrics and child health at Howard University medical school. From 1981 to 1985, Epps was project director for the Project to Consolidate Health Services for High Risk Young People. From 1985 to 1988, she was director of the Know Your Body Health Project.

Roselyn Epps has served as an international consultant for the World Bank, the U.N. Fund for Population, and the U.S. Department of Health and Human Services. She is a fellow of the American Academy of Pediatrics and has served as an officer of many organizations, including the National Medical Association, American Public Health Association, and American Medical Association.

Roselyn Payne Epps is married to Charles E. Epps, Jr., professor of orthopedic surgery and the dean of Howard University College of Medicine. They have four children.

SUSAN SHIFRIN

A practicing pediatrician, Roselyn Payne Epps is also an advocate for medical service for the poor, as well as a teacher, administrator, and organizational leader. (MEDICAL COLLEGE OF PENNSYLVANIA)

Evans, Matilda Arabella (1872–1935)

Matilda Arabella Evans was the first woman to be licensed to practice medicine in South Carolina. In her years of practice, she developed a model public school health testing program and founded a free health maintenance clinic, a hospital and training school, and a statewide health association.

Evans was born on May 13, 1872, in Aiken, South Carolina. Her parents were Anderson and Harriet Evans. Her maternal grandmother, Edith Corley, was the daughter of Henry and Julia Willis, who came from Pennsylvania.

Evans enrolled in the Schofield Industrial School in Aiken, South Carolina. The school was established in 1868 under the auspices of the Pennsylvania Farmers Relief Association to provide instruction to young black men and women.

At the urging of Martha Schofield, Evans enrolled in **Oberlin College.** Within three months she had won a scholarship to cover her tuition. To cover her other expenses she held a job as a waitress during the school year and canned fruit in the summer months. She attended Oberlin College from 1887 to 1891. Three months before her scheduled graduation, she dropped out of school to pursue a career in medicine. She taught briefly at the **Haines Institute** in Augusta, Georgia, and the Schofield School before enrolling at the Woman's Medical College of Pennsylvania in 1893.

Evans graduated from the Woman's Medical College in 1897 and returned to South Carolina to set up practice. She became a very successful surgeon who attracted both black and white patients. Her clientele grew so large that she opened her home as a hospital.

With the permission of South Carolina school authorities, Evans examined the health of black schoolchildren. She discovered that many of the children suffered from numerous ailments, including dental decay, infected tonsils, ringworm, and other diseases. As a result of her findings, the school district established a permanent health examination program within the public school system of South Carolina.

Evans was the founder of the Columbia Clinic Association in Columbia, South Carolina. The clinic was modeled after public health facilities that Evans had visited in Durham, North Carolina, Philadelphia, and New York City. The aim of the clinic was to teach families proper health maintenance while providing a variety of health services. All services at the clinic were provided free of charge.

In 1901, Evans established the Taylor Lane Hospital and Training School in Columbia. Although the city's population was 50 percent black, Taylor Lane Hospital was

The first woman licensed to practice medicine in South Carolina, Matilda Arabella Evans was active in community health and public school health issues, creating model testing programs and establishing a free public clinic, hospital and training school, and a statewide health association. (MEDICAL COLLEGE OF PENNSYLVANIA)

the only black hospital in the city. Evans gave up her private practice to work at the hospital. In addition to the services it provided black patients, the hospital proved to be an excellent training ground for black doctors and nurses.

Evans was not only a physician but also a great educator and humanitarian. She established the Negro Health Association of South Carolina to educate South Carolinians on proper health care procedures. She also provided recreation for underprivileged boys and formed swimming classes.

Evans received numerous honors and awards. She was given a commission from the National Council for Defense. She was elected president of the Palmetto State Medical Society, and was vice president of the National Medical Association. During World War I, she was appointed a member of the Volunteer Medical Service Corps.

Matilda Arabella Evans died at her home in Columbia, South Carolina, on November 17, 1935.

BRENDA GALLOWAY-WRIGHT

F

Ferebee, Dorothy (1898–1980)

Born in Norfolk, Virginia, in 1898, Dorothy Boulding was the daughter of Benjamin Richard and Florence Ruffin Boulding. She came from a family that included eight lawyers but no physicians. While her childhood friends were playing with toys, she would seek out and minister to injured birds and small dogs. Later, as a physician, her activities would include teaching, directing a university health service, and directing a mobile health clinic to serve patients who would not have received medical care otherwise.

Dorothy attended and graduated from Simmons College in Boston and pursued her medical education at nearby Tufts University School of Medicine. After graduating from Tufts in 1924, she went on to do her internship at Freedmen's Hospital in Washington, D.C. Freedmen's was one of the few hospitals that were owned and staffed by African Americans. Boulding completed her training, remained in Washington, D.C., and set up practice. She immediately became involved with numerous organizations and activities in Washington and nationally. In 1925, she joined the faculty of **Howard University** Medical School, and in 1949, she was appointed director of Howard's health services, a post she held until her retirement in 1968. She was the founding president of the Women's Institute, an organization that serves community groups, educational institutions, associations, industry, corporations, government agencies, nonprofit organizations, and individuals.

Dorothy Boulding married Claude Thurston Ferebee, a dentist and instructor in the Howard University College of Dentistry, in 1930. The next year, twins were born to them: a daughter named after Dorothy and a son named after Claude.

In 1934, Ferebee gained national prominence when she was appointed medical director of the Mississippi Health Project, sponsored by the **Alpha Kappa Alpha Sorority**. In this position, she directed the activities of mobile field units in neglected rural areas of Mississippi for seven years.

Active in the **National Council of Negro Women** (NCNW), she served as its second president from 1949 to 1953, following **Mary McLeod Bethune**. As NCNW president she worked toward expanding its programs aimed at eliminating discrimination against black Americans and women in the areas of health care education, housing, and the armed forces. She also proposed that the NCNW be active in expanding basic civil rights such as voting, fair employment, and education. Although she had the formidable task of following Bethune in this position, she was able to lead the NCNW ably while also carrying a full-time job.

She was a member of the American College Health Association, the National Medical Association, the American Association

71

A graduate of the Tufts University School of Medicine, Dorothy Ferebee gained national prominence in 1935 as the medical director of the Mississippi Health Project, which sent mobile health units into neglected rural areas of the state. Ferebee served as president of the National Council of Negro Women from 1949 to 1953. She is seen here (right) with two other NCNW presidents, Dorothy Height (center) and Vivian Carter Mason (left).
(BETHUNE MUSEUM AND ARCHIVES)

of University Women, and the National Council of Negro Women, to name a few.

Dorothy Boulding Ferebee died on September 14, 1980.

MARGARET JERRIDO

Fleetwood, Sara Iredell (1849–1908)

Sara Iredell Fleetwood, an educator and clubwoman, is best known for her involve-ment in the early black women's professional nursing movement. A native of Pennsylvania, Sara Iredell was born in April 1849. She remained active in the black community of Washington, D.C., until her death on February 1, 1908.

A graduate of the **Institute for Colored Youth** in Philadelphia, Iredell attended **Oberlin College,** as did several other black activist women at the turn of the twentieth century. After her graduation from Oberlin, where she was classified as a "pupil-teacher," Iredell began her teaching career in the Frederick, Maryland, public schools. Her dissatisfaction with the low pay and the treatment of black teachers there prompted her to seek a teaching position in the District of Columbia public schools for blacks. After a brief stint as a teacher, Sara Iredell Fleetwood devoted most of her adult professional life to the field of nursing.

In 1896, Fleetwood graduated in the first class of the Freedmen's Hospital Nursing Training School. Upon completing the nursing program, Fleetwood joined many of her fellow classmates in becoming a private nurse in Washington, D.C. Following the resignations of Sara C. Ebersole and her immediate successor in February 1901, Sara I. Fleetwood was appointed by the chief surgeon, Dr. Austin M. Curtis, as the first black superintendent of the hospital's nursing training school. In August of that same year, Fleetwood was reappointed by the new chief surgeon, Dr. William A. Warfield, and given the title of Directress of Nurses for Freedmen's Hospital. In 1904, Fleetwood resigned at the insistence of Warfield. According to W. Calvin Chase of the Washington *Bee,* her resignation was the result of a personal conflict with Warfield.

Her pioneer role as a black nurses' leader and educator extended beyond and after her years as a hospital administrator. Her interest in promoting the nursing profession and, in particular, greater black participation in the health care field, led her to organize the Freedmen's Nurses Association. In May 1904, she attended the seventh annual convention of the Nurses Association Alumnae of the United States as a delegate from the Freedmen's Association.

In recognition of her pioneer role in the nursing profession, Fleetwood became, in March 1907, the first and only black female appointed to the newly formed Nurses Examining Board of the District of Columbia. One of the chief responsibilities of the board was to certify registered nurses. Of the five women appointed, Fleetwood received the shortest term, ending in June 1907. She appealed to the District of Columbia commissioners to appoint as her replacement on the board someone who would represent the interests of Freedmen's Hospital in particular and the black community in general.

Her professional life overlapped with her active community role in the areas of black health and child care. As one of the nine original incorporators of a pioneer black women's club, the Colored Women's League of the District of Columbia (formed in 1892 and incorporated in 1894), Fleetwood concentrated on black family issues and health care. As did other educated league members, Fleetwood spoke at various public forums about various league projects and activities, ranging from day nurseries for working mothers to alley sanitation. "Motherhood—Its Relations to Race Development" was the title of the paper she delivered at the March 1891 meeting of the Bethel Literary and Historical Association. The 1898 annual report of the Colored Women's League included a testimonial to Fleetwood and her work as chairperson of the Mother's Meeting committee of the league, in which she focused on child care and parenting training for mothers.

Fleetwood, along with another prominent league member, Anna E. Murray, represented the Colored Women's League at the 1898 Congress of Mothers. Three years earlier, she was one of the league's delegates to the 1895 triennial meeting of the predominantly white National Council of Women.

Fleetwood combined her active civic and professional life with her responsibilities as a wife and mother. Like Sara, her husband, Civil War hero Christian A. Fleetwood, whom she married in 1869, was an active member of the Washington black community. Together they had one daughter, Edith, who continued the family tradition of community service. The family resided for many years on Spruce Street in the northwest neighborhood of LeDroit Park. Originally an all-white neighborhood, it soon became home to a large enclave of black professionals.

Sara Iredell Fleetwood symbolized the black professional woman of her day in that she was equally dedicated to her professional nursing career and to the black women's clubs she joined. It was important to these educated, middle-class women to bring the value of their education and training to the persons whom they identified as being the less fortunate members of their race.

SHARON HARLEY

Ford, Justina (1871–1952)

Justina Ford was the first African-American woman physician to live and work in the Denver, Colorado, area.

Born on January 22, 1871, in Knoxville, Illinois, Justina grew up in Galesburg, Illinois. Her mother was a nurse, and she was the seventh child in the family. She would not play with her siblings unless they played hospital and she was the doctor.

Following her graduation in 1899 from the Hering Medical School in Chicago, Illinois, she directed a hospital in Normal, Alabama, for two years. Then she moved to Denver in 1902. She applied for her license and found the authorities reluctant to grant it to her because she was an African-American woman. However, she did

Dr. Justina Ford was one the first black women physicians in the Rocky Mountain west. (BLACK AMERICAN WEST MUSEUM AND HERITAGE CENTER)

get her license and set up her practice. Still, the medical community was slow to recognize her abilities. Ford was not accepted into membership by the Denver Medical Society, the Colorado Medical Society, or the American Medical Association until very late in her life.

Specializing in obstetrics, gynecology, and pediatrics, she came to be known as the "baby doctor." Because Denver General Hospital would not take black patients or physicians, Ford took her practice door-to-door. A stern and brisk-mannered woman, Ford was known for her unique system of delivering and providing the best care for mother and baby in the home. She delivered over 7,000 babies before, during, and after World War II. Her patients came from many ethnic groups including those of Hispanic, Native American, Chinese, Greek, Japanese, African-American, and European origin. Transportation to her patients progressed from horse and buggy to taxicabs. She finally purchased a car and hired a relative to drive her. When her car came into a neighborhood, it was a sure sign that someone was having a baby.

Justina married Reverend Ford early in her career. She remarried after her first husband's death, but she continued to be known as Dr. Ford. Her second husband was Alfred Allen.

She succeeded in being admitted as a staff member of the Denver General Hospital, the same hospital that had refused her services early in her career. Moreover, her home and office have been relocated, renovated, and reopened as the permanent headquarters of the Black American West Museum in Denver, Colorado. It is also used as a community meeting place.

Ford died at the age of eighty-one in October 1952.

MARGARET JERRIDO

Franklin, Martha Minerva (1870–1968)

Prior to the founding of the **National Association of Colored Graduate Nurses** (NACGN) in 1908, black women were outcasts in the nursing profession. Martha Minerva Franklin resolved to change the status of black nurses and so founded the NACGN.

Born on October 29, 1870, in New Milford, Connecticut, to Henry J. Franklin and Mary E. Gauson Franklin, Martha graduated from Meriden Public High School in 1890. Five years later she entered the Woman's Hospital Training School for Nurses in Philadelphia, one of the few black women to have access to such a nursing program. The vast majority of nursing schools either severely restricted or prohibited the admission of black women. This widespread system of racial discrimination and exclusion propelled many African Americans to found a separate black network of health care institutions and nurse training schools.

The sole black student in her class, Franklin received her diploma in December 1897. She found employment as a private-duty nurse, hospital staff or public health nursing seldom being available to black nurses. Franklin worked for a while in Meriden and then in New Haven.

As a graduate nurse, she was confronted by the unjust treatment of black nurses. The denial of admission to hospital nursing schools limited the number of black trained nurses, and those few who did graduate were denied membership in the American Nurses Association (ANA), since membership in a state nurses' association was a prerequisite to membership in the ANA, and all Southern state associations barred black women.

In fall 1906, Franklin launched an investigation of the status of black graduate nurses. She discovered widespread dissatisfaction among black nurses, coupled with an eagerness to improve themselves professionally. Franklin and the black nurses who responded to her survey recognized the need to unite in order to promote racial integration and to achieve greater acceptance within their profession.

Adah Belle Samuels Thoms, president of the Lincoln Hospital School of Nursing Alumnae Association, responded to one of the 1,500 letters Franklin wrote. Thoms invited Franklin and interested nurses to meet in New York City as guests of the association. In August 1908, fifty-two nurses attended a meeting chaired by Franklin. During the three-day conference, the participants reached a consensus about the need to form a permanent professional organization. Out of this meeting emerged the National Association of Colored Graduate Nurses, with twenty-six charter members. In light of her initiative and leadership, the group unanimously elected Franklin president. She was re-elected in 1909. When she declined to serve a third term, the members designated her honorary president for life and made her the NACGN's permanent historian.

During the 1920s, Franklin relocated to New York City. She enrolled in a six-month postgraduate course at Lincoln Hospital, became a registered nurse, and found employment as a nurse in the New York City public school system. Considering education to be a lifelong pursuit, at the age of fifty-eight she studied at Teachers College, Columbia University, in the Department of Practical Arts, now the Department of Nursing Education. She died on September 26, 1968.

DARLENE CLARK HINE

G

Gilbert, Artishia Garcia (b. 1869)

Artishia Gilbert, the first black woman to pass the medical boards and register as a physician in Kentucky, had an extraordinary educational career. The daughter of an itinerant miner, she graduated in 1885, at the age of sixteen, from the State Normal and Theological Institute and then earned a B.A. from the State University of Kentucky. Three years later, in 1892, Gilbert completed her M.A. at that school and went on to earn a medical degree from the Louisville National Medical College, even while she traveled and lectured extensively for the Baptist Educational Convention.

Seeking further training, she moved to Washington, D.C., and entered the medical program at **Howard University,** from which she graduated in 1897. Shortly thereafter, she married John Wilkerson, a Louisville lawyer, and accepted a position as teaching assistant in obstetrics at the State University of Kentucky. She served also as superintendent of the Red Cross Sanitarium and on the board of Orphans Home in Louisville.

GLORIA MOLDOW

Gilmer, Gloria (19??–)

Dr. Gloria Gilmer is one of the very few people familiar with all the levels of mathematics education, from nursery school to graduate school. A dynamic innovator, she is president of Math-Tech, a corporation (established 1984) in Milwaukee, Wisconsin, that translates research findings into effective programs in mathematics education, especially for women and minorities.

Since 1985, she has chaired both the International Study Group on Ethno-mathematics and the Committee on Opportunities in Mathematics for Underrepresented Minorities. The latter is a joint endeavor of three scholarly societies that together organized a series of national conferences. "Making Mathematics Work for Minorities," as these were entitled in 1989 and 1990, included six regional conferences and a national conference, for which Gilmer served on the steering committee.

She was the first black female (1980–82) to sit on the board of governors of the Mathematical Association of America (MAA); thereafter, the board decided to appoint and continue to appoint a governor-at-large for minorities. During the same years she was national director of the MAA speakers' program, "Blacks and Mathematics." From 1981 to 1985, she chaired an MAA panel on remediation.

Always exploring varied ways of learning and teaching mathematics, Gilmer gave a speech on worldwide developments in ethnomathematics at the Sixth International Congress on Mathematical Education in Budapest, Hungary, in July 1988. She was a member of the U.S. mathematics delegation to the People's Republic of China in 1983 and of the mathematics educators' study tour of the Soviet Union in 1988.

Gilmer was a research associate with the U.S. Department of Education (1981–84) and is a former mathematician in exterior ballistics with the U.S. Army at Aberdeen Proving Grounds. She has served on the mathematics faculties of six traditionally black institutions of higher education and taught mathematics at the Milwaukee Area Technical College (1965–79) and in the Milwaukee public schools (1959–65).

Born in Baltimore, Maryland, to Mittie and James Ford, she holds B.S. and M.A. degrees in mathematics from Morgan State University and the University of Pennsylvania, respectively. Her Ph.D. in curriculum and instruction is from Marquette University. Gilmer is married and has two children. Her son is a lawyer and her daughter, who holds an M.B.A., is vice president of Math-Tech.

Mathematics educator and president of Math-Tech, Gloria Gilmer utilizes her warmth and humor, as well as her intellect, to improve the working relationship between mathematics and black women. (PATRICIA KENSCHAFT)

Without Gloria Gilmer's energetic and imaginative contributions, the U.S. mathematics community would be far less diverse and welcoming. For example, it was she who suggested the staging of skits dramatizing micro-inequities to facilitate mathematicians' self-examination; hundreds of mathematicians have flocked to these skits and discussed them widely. Her lively humor and warm compassion complement her visionary perspective and her commitment to social change.

PATRICIA CLARK KENSCHAFT

Granville, Evelyn Boyd (1924–)

"I . . . have had a very rich life. I have been blessed with a fine family, an excellent education, many friends . . . and last, but by no means least, a happy (second) marriage." One of the first two black women to earn a Ph.D. in mathematics (the other is **Marjorie Lee Browne**), Evelyn Boyd Granville's pioneering career and warm personality have inspired many.

She was born Evelyn Boyd on May 1, 1924, to William and Julia Walker Boyd in Washington, D.C. She and her older sister were raised primarily by their mother and their mother's twin sister, Louise Walker. After graduating from Dunbar High School in Washington, D.C., she won a partial scholarship to Smith College. She was able to afford her college education by living in a cooperative, by working summers at the National Bureau of Standards, and through the financial help she received from her mother and aunt. In 1945, she graduated summa cum laude and was elected to Phi Beta Kappa.

She won awards for graduate study at Yale University, including a Smith College fellowship, a Julius Rosenwald fellowship, and an Atomic Energy Commission fellowship. In 1949, she received her doctorate with a specialty in functional analysis, and she was elected to the scientific honorary society, Sigma Xi.

Although her advisor at Yale was a former president of the American Mathematical Society and her academic credentials were impeccable, she could not find a university with a Ph.D. program that would hire her. She taught for two years at Fisk University, inspiring at least two younger women (Etta Falconer and Vivienne Malone Mayes) to obtain Ph.D.s in mathematics. In 1952, she became an applied mathematician at the Diamond Ordnance Fuze Laboratories, and in 1956 she joined IBM to work on the formulation of orbit computations and computer procedures for the Project Vanguard and Project Mercury space probes.

She then participated in research studies on the methods of orbit computation, with the Computation and Data Reduction Center of the U.S. Space Technology Laboratories. Later she became a research specialist in celestial mechanics, trajectory and orbit computation, numerical analysis, and digital computer techniques, for Apollo engineers at the North American Aviation Space and Information Systems Division. This was followed by four more years with IBM as a senior mathematician.

In 1967, she joined the faculty of California State University in Los Angeles, from which she retired as a full professor in 1984. She and her husband bought a sixteen-acre farm in Texas, where they raised

Space beckoned mathematician Evelyn Boyd Granville as she worked on orbit computations and computer procedures for Project Vanguard and Project Mercury. (PATRICIA KENSCHAFT)

chickens. From 1985 to 1988, she taught mathematics and computer science full time at Texas College in Tyler. In 1990, she was appointed to the Sam A. Lindsey Chair at the University of Texas at Tyler.

Evelyn Boyd Granville was a member of the U.S. Civil Service Panel of Examiners of the Department of Commerce (1954–56); the psychology examining committee of the Board of Medical Examiners of the State of California (1963–70); an advisory committee of the National Defense Education Act Title IV Graduate Fellowship Program of the Office of Education (1966–69); and the board of trustees of the Center for the Improvement of Mathematics Education in San Diego (1975–79). She has been active in the National Council of Teachers of Mathematics and the California Mathematics Council. She was president of the Beverly Hills branch of the American Association of University Women from 1968 to 1970. In 1989, she became the first black woman mathematician to receive an honorary doctorate when Smith College, her undergraduate alma mater, bestowed one on her.

PATRICIA CLARK KENSCHAFT

Born into slavery, Eliza Anna Grier triumphed to become the first black woman to be licensed to practice medicine in the state of Georgia. (MEDICAL COLLEGE OF PENNSYLVANIA)

Grier, Eliza Anna (1864–1902)

Eliza Anna Grier was born in North Carolina in July 1864. A former slave, she was the first black woman physician to be licensed to practice medicine in the state of Georgia. In 1884, she enrolled in the Normal Course at Fisk University, in Nashville, Tennessee. Because of financial difficulties, it took her seven years to complete her degree.

Following her graduation from Fisk University in 1891, Grier taught school for one year at the Paine Normal School and Industrial Institute (now Paine College) in Augusta, Georgia. In 1893, she matriculated at the Woman's Medical College of Pennsylvania. During the 1894–95 session she received a $100 stipend to cover some of her medical school costs. She graduated from the Woman's Medical College in 1897.

Grier set up practice in Greenville, South Carolina. Letters written by Grier in 1901 alluded to the fact that her practice was not very successful and that she was in need of financial assistance. She died of a stroke on April 14, 1902. She is buried in Charlotte, North Carolina.

BRENDA GALLOWAY-WRIGHT

Hale, Mamie Odessa (1911–c. 1968)

Born in Pennsylvania in 1911, Mamie Odessa Hale attended teachers college to become a registered public health nurse. After working as a public health nurse in Pittsburgh, Hale attended the Tuskegee School of Nurse-Midwifery for Colored Nurses in Alabama. Graduating with a certificate in midwifery, she was recruited by the Arkansas State Board of Health to assist with maternal-child health programs.

From 1945 to 1950, Nurse Hale's primary task was to train black granny midwives to safely deliver the babies of Arkansas' black women. Almost all the black babies in Arkansas were delivered at home without medical supervision, resulting in very high death rates among black women and their babies.

The task for Nurse Hale, as she was called by everyone, was particularly challenging. Granny midwives managed the deliveries, and almost 75 percent of them were illiterate. Most were elderly, between sixty and eighty, and reluctant to change their ways. Undaunted by the mission ahead of her, and driven by the desire to prevent other deaths, Nurse Hale organized a series of classes for these granny midwives to improve their knowledge of and skill in midwifery.

Nurse Hale taught the midwives through songs, movies, and demonstration methods. She would simulate a birth, to teach midwives how to care for the pregnant woman before, during, and after the delivery. She assembled a book full of illustrations to teach midwives about what they

From 1945 to 1950, pioneer educator Mamie Hale taught Arkansas midwives how to deliver babies at home safely. The State Board of Health required all midwives to take her program. The death rate for Arkansas' black women and babies fell from 76 deaths in 1940 to 43 in 1950. (UNIVERSITY OF ARKANSAS FOR MEDICAL SCIENCES)

needed to take to deliveries. In the midwife bag were all the necessary items for a safe delivery. There were clean newspapers to protect the woman's bed, string to tie the baby's cord, dressings for the cord stub, and ampules of silver nitrate and cotton balls for the baby's eyes.

The State Board of Health required all midwives to take the program and be awarded a permit to deliver babies. By 1950, just over 1,000 midwives had such permits in Arkansas. The death rate for Arkansas' black women and babies fell from 76 deaths in 1940 to 43 in 1950. Mamie Hale's efforts had resulted in dramatic improvements in the quality of obstetrical care in Arkansas.

PEGGE BELL

Hale, Millie E. (1881–1930)

When it comes to providing health care and social services for African Americans, few can come close to the extraordinary achievements of Millie E. Hale. An early twentieth-century visionary, Hale's sense of social activism inspired her to found a hospital, a nursing school, and a community center, and to serve the needs of the poor of Nashville, Tennessee, on an unprecedented level.

Millie E. Hale was born in Nashville on February 27, 1891, one of five children of Henry and Nannie Gibson. In 1901, she graduated from Fisk University's Normal School, then went on to study nursing at the Graduate School for Nurses in New York City. She earned a bachelor's degree from Fisk University in 1927.

Determined to improve health care for Nashville's African-American community,

Hale founded the Millie E. Hale Hospital in 1916. The hospital was a landmark, the first year-round hospital in the city for African Americans. It was a relatively small institution at first, where she, her husband—notable physician John Henry Hale—and a small staff cared for patients in twelve beds. The hospital quickly became known for its first-rate health care and, within five years, it grew to one hundred beds served by a staff of twenty-six nurses and five physicians.

Hale recognized, however, the link between health issues and larger questions of social need in the community. She became a driving force behind the hospital's movement into social service, providing free medical and surgical care to the poor and relief to families of the sick, and even publishing a monthly newspaper focusing on the health needs of the African-American community. She worked to develop the hospital's nurse training department, and by 1925 twenty-four women had graduated from its three-year program. Its reputation growing, the Millie E. Hale Hospital was recognized for excellence by the American College of Surgeons.

Millie Hale's drive to help the community extended beyond her work at the hospital, however. She and her husband converted their house into a community center, providing free health lectures, prenatal care, a free clinic for the needy, and a meeting place for black women. She purchased land for the development of four large playgrounds for children and sponsored free picnics, band concerts, and open-air movies for Nashville's young people. In addition, Hale managed a community grocery store.

Hale was active in community activities and organizations, including the St. Paul African Methodist Episcopal Church, the YWCA, the Nashville Federation of Colored Women's Clubs, and the Heliotrope Literary Circle.

On June 6, 1930, Millie E. Hale died in the hospital that she founded. Her accomplishments, however, live on.

CHRISTINE SUMPTION

Hall, Julia R. (b. 1865)

Julia Hall's career spanned more than fifty years and involved a variety of medical practices. In 1889, she came with her husband, Reverend Jeremiah M. Hall, to the District of Columbia and entered the **Howard University** medical program the following year. She graduated in 1892 and entered the practice of medicine. She was appointed resident to the gynecology clinic at Howard—the first woman at that school to receive such an appointment—and for many years served as matron and medical advisor to the girls at Miner's Hall at Howard University. Hall also was distinguished by being the first woman to be appointed to the Board of Children's Guardians in the capital.

GLORIA MOLDOW

Hewitt, Gloria Conyers (1935–)

"They were so busy loving me that they didn't notice that they didn't respect me— so, of course, neither did I," said mathematician Gloria Conyers Hewitt of her all-male, all-white colleagues at the University of Montana at Missoula in the mid-1970s. One of them had recommended her for a merit award, her department had supported her, but the dean had denied the award.

In preparation for an appeal, she was asked if she could prove that the widespread recognition she had received was not *just* because of her sex/race. "Nobody around here knew more math than me," she remembered in a 1991 interview. "They weren't doing that much research either. One day I got mad. 'I don't care what you think,' I said, and I meant it. 'I'm tired of trying to please you. What you think of me doesn't matter to me any more.' Then they *had* to begin *respecting* me. I believe

One of the first black women to receive the Ph.D. in mathematics, Gloria Conyers Hewitt has served for many years on the Educational Testing Service's Graduate Record Examination Committee. (PATRICIA KENSCHAFT)

now that my colleagues both respect and like me." Eleven years after she was denied the aforementioned merit award, she received one initiated by the dean. Now she chairs the graduate committee, and was asked to consider becoming the department chair. She declined.

Gloria Conyers was born to Crenella and Emmett Conyers, Sr., in Sumter, South Carolina, on October 26, 1935. She attended Fisk University from 1952 to 1956. There she took mathematics courses from Lee Lorch, who, though he was dismissed at the end of her second year, had recommended her for graduate study without consulting her. She was amazed when in her senior year she was offered a fellowship at the University of Washington in Seattle without applying for it. But she accepted it.

In 1962, she became the third black woman in the United States to receive a Ph.D. in mathematics. In fall 1961, she joined the faculty of the University of Montana in Missoula. She became a full professor in 1972.

She was a visiting lecturer for the Mathe-matical Association of America from 1964 to 1972, giving lectures and colloquia at many institutions. She was on the executive council of Pi Mu Epsilon, the mathematical honor society from 1972 to 1975. From 1976 to 1986, she was a member of Educational Testing Service's Graduate Record Examination Committee, which planned and made up questions for the subject test in mathematics. From 1984 to 1986, she chaired this committee. She served on the College Board's Advanced Placement Calculus Development Committee from 1987 to 1991, planning questions for the AP calculus examination.

In 1980–81, she spent a sabbatical year at Case Institute, studying algebraic topology and homological algebra. She has taught a course and supervised a doctoral dissertation in homological algebra at the University of Montana. She coauthored a publication with a student, a copy of which she saw at the mathematical institute in Beijing when she visited there with the Women in Mathematics tour of China in 1990.

PATRICIA CLARK KENSCHAFT

J

Jackson, Shirley Ann (1946–)

Shirley Ann Jackson is a theoretical physicist. One of the most distinguished young black scientists in the country today, she commands respect in a profession overwhelmingly populated by white males. As a theorist, Jackson uses mathematics to predict the behavior of subatomic particles.

Born on August 5, 1946, in Washington, D.C., Jackson is the daughter of George and Beatrice Jackson. Both her parents believed strongly in education, and encouraged her in school. Her father helped her build science fair experiments, which helped establish her interest in science. Jackson was part of an accelerated program in science and mathematics at Roosevelt High School, which gave her a solid foundation on which to build. She graduated as valedictorian from Roosevelt in 1964.

Jackson next entered the Massachusetts Institute of Technology, one of the top technological universities in the nation. In 1968, she was awarded the S.B. degree in physics. She continued at the same school for her graduate work and, in 1973, became the first black woman to receive a Ph.D. from M.I.T. Her field was theoretical elementary particle physics. Her work was directed by James Young, the first full-time, tenured, black professor in the M.I.T. department of physics.

Jackson won a number of grants and fellowships while at M.I.T, including a National Science Foundation Traineeship (1968–71) and a Ford Foundation Advanced Study Fellowship (1971–73). After graduating, she received a Ford Foundation Individual Grant. While a student at M.I.T, Jackson volunteered at Boston City Hospital and tutored at the Roxbury YMCA.

After completing her Ph.D., Jackson became a research associate at the Fermi National Accelerator Laboratory near Chicago. She served two terms there, from 1973 to 1974, and from 1974 to 1976. In the 1970s, she also spent a considerable amount of time studying at some of the most important research facilities in Europe.

Jackson is a theoretical physicist, which means that she and her colleagues work out mathematical models that predict what will happen on a subatomic level. Unlike many natural phenomena, such as animals, plants, and weather patterns, subatomic particles are too difficult to study without structures and expectations. They require elaborate experiments with rare and highly specialized equipment.

Therefore, theorists such as Jackson work out mathematical models to predict the behavior of the particles in question. They then turn over their theories to experimental physicists, who design and run experiments to prove or disprove the theories. Jackson's particular interest is in the way the components of atoms interact with each other. In this way scientists learn about the basic qualities of matter, which can affect everything from new sources of energy to the creation of new household products.

Since 1976, Jackson has been employed at the AT&T Bell Laboratories at Murray Hill, New Jersey. In 1985, she was appointed by the governor of New Jersey to the New Jersey Commission on Science and Technology. She was reappointed for a five-year term in 1989.

In 1986, in recognition of her contributions to research, Jackson was elected a Fellow of the American Physical Society. She also has served on committees for the National Science Foundation, National Academy of Sciences, and American Association for the Advancement of Science. Jackson has received numerous awards and honors. She is on the governing board of the American Institute of Physics, and is a member of a half-dozen other professional societies. She has published more than 100 scientific articles and abstracts.

Jackson may have been one of the first black women to become a theoretical physicist, but she does not intend to be the last. She has been instrumental in inspiring other black women scientists to seek out exciting research in difficult fields. Of all her many accomplishments, one of the finest has been her determination to open new fields to the contributions of black women scientists.

ANDRA MEDEA

Johnson, Halle Tanner (1864–1901)

"[I] try to keep before [myself] the possibility of failing but unless some harder and more complex than anything they have given me yet I feel that I can not, but, if they mark me fairly, get thro." With this

Halle Tanner Johnson was an Alabama pioneer: the first black woman to sit for—and pass—a medical board examination, and the first woman of any race to be licensed to practice medicine in the state. As resident physician at Tuskegee Institute, she established a nurses' training school and a dispensary to care for the needs of the community as well as the campus population. (MEDICAL COLLEGE OF PENNSYLVANIA)

determination and self-confidence, Halle Tanner Dillon passed the state medical examinations in Alabama in 1891 and became the first woman to be licensed to practice medicine in the state. Her concern for social justice led her to establish a training school and dispensary at Tuskegee Institute in Alabama, where she became resident physician.

Halle (Hallie) Tanner was born in Pittsburgh, Pennsylvania, on October 17, 1864, to Benjamin Tucker Tanner and Sarah Elizabeth (Miller) Tanner. She was the eldest daughter of nine children, two of whom died in infancy. The Tanners were a prominent family whose home in Philadelphia was a rest haven for travelers and a meeting place for black intellectuals, including leading black and white clergy. The parents created a culturally developed and intellectually stimulating atmosphere, introducing their children to the works of prominent African-American artists such as Edward Bannister and Edmonia Lewis. The Tanners' son, Henry Ossawa (1859–1937), was guided by the experience; the gifted artist became a celebrated painter of landscape, religious, and genre paintings.

Benjamin Tucker Tanner, a successful minister in the African Methodist Episcopal (AME) Church, edited the *Christian Recorder* beginning in 1868; he was first editor of the *AME Church Review* in 1884 and two years later was elected a bishop in the church. He had worked incessantly on the *Review,* with daughter Halle as an office staff member. She soon met Charles E. Dillon, of Trenton, New Jersey, and after a brief courtship they married in the Tanner home in June 1886. Halle gave birth to the Dillons' only child, Sadie, in 1887. The marriage ended with Charles Dillon's death, although the details and date of death are unknown. Halle Dillon and her daughter returned to the Tanner home on Diamond Street, where they remained for several months.

Determined to put her life back in order, Dillon, then twenty-four years old, enrolled in the Woman's Medical College of Pennsylvania. The only black student in her class of thirty-six women, she completed the three-year course and graduated with high honors on May 7, 1891. Booker T. Washington, president of Tuskegee Institute, had searched for four years for a black resident physician to provide health care for the local community. He had written to the dean of the Woman's Medical College for a nomination, who apparently mentioned it to Dillon. Dillon was interested in the position and wrote to Washington.

Washington's letters to Halle Dillon introduced her to the social and economic climate in Tuskegee and the responsibilities of the position. Washington preferred a black woman, and he offered a salary of $600 a year with board included. The resident physician would teach two classes each day, administer the health department, and compound the medicines needed to serve the sick. Additional compensation was to be derived from the physician's private practice. Much of the work would be missionary in spirit; thus, the physician would need to sign on for the good of the cause. The physician would need to pass the local or state medical examination and begin work on September 1, 1891.

Halle Dillon found the offer appealing, accepted the challenge, and arrived in Tuskegee in August 1891. Washington had arranged for her to prepare for the strenuous medical board examination through study with Cornelius Nathaniel Dorsett, a practicing physician in Montgomery where the examinations were to be held. Dorsett was the first black physician to pass the Alabama medical board. Both Bishop Tanner and Halle Dillon were confident of Dillon's ability to pass any reasonable and just examination; however, they were more concerned about the examining board. Halle Dillon's impending appearance before the examiners caused a public stir. Some questioned her daring to sit for the examination. The curious wanted to know how she looked.

The ten-day examinations tested her on a separate subject each day. At the end, the board supervisor was impressed with Halle Dillon's neatness and cleanliness in work. Three weeks after her return to Tuskegee, she learned that she had passed with an average of 78.81. Confident of her accuracy and completeness in response to the examination questions, Dillon felt that the examiner might have been too critical and too rigid in evaluating her papers.

The press took notice of Dillon's success and acknowledged her to be the first woman of any race to become licensed as a medical doctor in Alabama and the first black woman to practice medicine in the state. Dillon's achievement also called attention to a double standard regarding the races, for Anna M. Longshore, a white woman who failed the medical examination earlier, had practiced medicine in Alabama without a license before Dillon took the test.

From 1891 to 1894, Halle Dillon was resident physician at Tuskegee. During this time she established a nurses' training school and the Lafayette Dispensary to provide for the health care needs of the local residents and the campus. She also compounded many of her own medicines. In 1894, she married Reverend John Quincy Johnson, who in 1893–94 was a mathematics teacher at Tuskegee. The next year, John Quincy Johnson became president of Allen University, a private school for black students in Columbia, South Carolina. He

received a B.D. from Hartford Divinity School, Hartford, Connecticut, and the D.D. from Morris Brown College, Atlanta, Georgia. Halle Johnson joined her husband when he did postgraduate work at Princeton Theological Seminary.

The Johnsons moved to Nashville, Tennessee, where John Quincy Johnson was pastor of Saint Paul AME Church from 1900 to 1903. They had three sons, who were named after their noted father, grandfather, and uncle: John Quincy, Jr., Benjamin T., and Henry Tanner. Complications of childbirth and dysentery led to Halle Johnson's death in her Nashville home on April 26, 1901, when she was thirty-seven years old. She is buried in Nashville's Greenwood Cemetery. Three grandchildren and two grandnieces survive her today.

Halle Tanner Dillon Johnson, a member of a noted and highly respected black family of the nineteenth century, is a notable figure in black and American history and in the racial history of the South. She became an Alabama pioneer when she became the first woman in the state to pass the medical board examination. She withstood the curiosity of a questioning society that had not seen a black woman sit for a medical examination; she opened public discussion of racial discrimination in the medical profession; and she improved significantly the health care of a racially segregated community by providing training for nurses, building a dispensary, and ministering to the needs of the residents.

JESSIE CARNEY SMITH

Johnson, Hazel Winifred (1927–)

Interested in travel and changing her outlook, Hazel Johnson entered the army in

1955, five years after completing basic nurses' training at New York's Harlem Hospital. She received a direct commission as a first lieutenant in the U.S. Army Nursing Corps in May 1960. Nineteen years later, the one-star insignia, representing brigadier general, was pinned on her uniform. Thus, at age fifty-two, Hazel Winifred Johnson became the first black woman general in the history of the U.S. military.

Taking advantage of the educational opportunities provided by the military, she earned a bachelor's degree in nursing from Villanova University, a master's degree in nursing education from Columbia University, and a Ph.D. in education administration through Catholic University. She was chief of the Army Nurse Corps from 1979 to 1983, the first black American to hold the corps' most powerful position. The promotion to brigadier general was recommended by a military board and approved by Congress.

In 1983, the general retired and rejoined civilian life as director of the government affairs division of the American Nurses Association. Three years later, she left to assume a professorship of nursing at George Mason University in Virginia. Her retirement from the army created a void in top female leadership, leaving only two women generals, neither of whom was black. After Hazel Johnson's retirement, two years elapsed before another black woman, in any branch of the military, pinned on the coveted star: **Sheridan G. Cadoria.**

Although retired from army service, military mementos adorn the Clifton, Virginia, home of Johnson and her husband, David Brown. The Distinguished Service Medal, the Legion of Merit, the Meritorious Service Medal, and an Army Commendation Medal with an oak leaf cluster are among the general's decorations, awards, and badges.

LINDA ROCHELL LANE

Johnson, Katherine (1918–)

An aerospace technologist, Katherine Johnson went from a farm in West Virginia to the stars, going around, past, or through many "no coloreds" and "whites only" signs to get there.

Katherine Johnson grew up in a family that put education first. Her father would move the family into town during the school year, because he believed that his children should go to high school. Johnson attended West Virginia State College, where she studied French, physics, and mathematics. She became a teacher after graduation and taught public school for several years.

In 1953, at the age of thirty-five, Katherine Johnson felt she needed a career change, and she joined the staff at the National Advisory Committee on Aviation (NASA's predecessor). At first, she worked in the "black workers' pool" at the racially segregated government organization. Then she found herself "loaned out" to the Flight Research Division. She never looked back.

Her first job at Flight Research was to interpret data from the computers of very early prototypes of a spacecraft—called "pilotless aircraft." She stayed with the division and worked on the Apollo Project, calculating flight trajectories for the different missions and developing the project's emergency navigational methods, to be used in case the spaceship lost contact with ground control. She is considered a pioneer in developing practical methods of tracking space missions. Johnson analyzed data gathered at tracking stations around the globe.

During the lunar orbital missions that were known as the "moon shots," along with more than a dozen other black scientists, she worked on Project Mercury with Lt. Col. John Glenn. For her pioneering work in the field, she received the Group Achievement Award, presented to NASA's Lunar Spacecraft and Operations team.

Katherine Johnson retired from NASA in 1986, after thirty years of service with the space program. She was there from before the beginning through the space shuttle. She developed flight plans for ships that were considered to be science fiction by most people at the time. She may have had to ride at the back of the bus to get to work, but we're very lucky she got there.

HILARY MAC AUSTIN

Jones, Sarah Garland (d. 1905)

Sarah Garland Jones, the first woman to be licensed to practice medicine in the state of Virginia, was born in Albemarle County, Virginia, soon after the end of the Civil War. Her parents were Ellen and George W. Boyd. George Boyd was a distinguished black contractor and builder in Richmond.

Sarah Jones attended public school in Richmond and graduated from the Richmond Normal School in 1883, after which she taught locally for nearly five years. In 1888, she married Miles Berkley Jones, then secretary of the True Reformers. Her desire to pursue a medical career prompted her to resign her teaching position and

enter Howard Medical School in 1890. Following her graduation in 1893, she passed the Virginia State Board examinations, which granted her the right to practice medicine in the state. She and her husband, also a physician, operated a lucrative practice in Richmond for many years and were well respected within the black community.

In 1898, the Joneses founded a patient-care facility called the Women's Central Hospital and Richmond Hospital. The hospital had twenty-five beds and catered primarily to the needs of female patients. A training school for nurses was affiliated with the hospital in 1901, graduating its first class that same year. Incorporated in 1912, the hospital changed its name to the Sarah Jones Memorial Hospital. The school stayed open until 1920.

At the time of her death in 1905, Jones was still the only black woman practicing medicine in the state of Virginia.

BRENDA GALLOWAY-WRIGHT

Jones, Sophia Bethene (1857–1932)

Born in Ontario, Canada, in 1857, Sophia Bethene Jones entered the University of Toronto in 1879. Around 1881, she came to the United States and studied medicine at the University of Michigan. After she graduated in 1885, Jones went to **Spelman College** in Atlanta, Georgia. She became the first black woman to teach at Spelman and was in charge of the college infirmary and setting up a nurses' training course. She taught there from 1885 to 1888.

Sophia Jones also practiced in St. Louis, Philadelphia, and Kansas. While in Kansas, her health began to fail, and she moved to California with her brothers and sisters. She lived for fifteen more years and died in 1932.

MARGARET JERRIDO

Jones, Verina Morton (1865–1943)

Physician, clubwoman, civil rights activist, and suffragist, Verina Morton-Jones was born in Cleveland, Ohio, on January 28, 1865. She attended State Normal School in Columbia, South Carolina, and later the Woman's Medical College of Pennsylvania in Philadelphia—then widely acknowledged to be one of the best medical colleges for women in the country—from 1884 to 1888. She received her M.D. in 1888 and began to practice in the black community surrounding Rust College in Holly Springs, Mississippi. Morton-Jones was the first woman, black or white, to practice medicine in the state of Mississippi. She married twice; the first time in 1890 to W. A. Morton, M.D., who died in 1895, and the second time in 1901 to Emory Jones, who died in 1927. She had one child from her first marriage, Franklin W., who was born in 1892.

Among the first black women in the U.S. to receive a degree in medicine, Morton-Jones moved to New York to practice in Brooklyn and on Long Island during the Progressive Era. She was the first black woman to practice medicine in Nassau County on Long Island, and she played an active role in the largely white, male-dominated Kings County Medical Society. In the 1941–44 edition of *Who's Who in Colored America,* Morton-Jones is described as "the oldest colored physician in

The distinguished Verina Morton was the first woman, black or white, to practice medicine in the state of Mississippi, but her greatest achievement was her leadership of the Lincoln Settlement House in Brooklyn, which offered, among other services, a clinic and a day nursery and free kindergarten. (MOORLAND-SPINGARN)

Brooklyn in point of practice as well as age." In spite of her long and active career in medicine and healing, Morton-Jones also devoted her time to club work, education, suffrage, community "uplift," and civil rights.

Morton-Jones headed the Lincoln Settlement House in Brooklyn from its founding in May 1908. Lincoln House began as an extension of white social reformer and nurse Lillian Wald's Henry Street Settlement House on the Lower East Side of New York City. The primary sponsor of this self-help, community-based program, Morton-Jones contributed the down payment on the property for the settlement house and pioneered the first social service organization in Brooklyn that sought to address the needs of the growing black population.

Under her directorship, Lincoln House offered a clinic, a day nursery, and free kindergarten; a lecture series on health and hygiene; and classes in carpentry, cooking, embroidery, folk dancing, and sewing. It also sponsored choral and debating clubs. It appealed not only to black youth but also to the adults of the community. The settlement house incorporated in 1914 and moved from its original quarters at 129 Willoughby Street to 105 Fleet Place, where there was a more spacious building and a nearby lot for a playground.

Morton-Jones nurtured diverse social and political commitments. As a black clubwoman, she played an active part in the **National Association of Colored Women** (NACW, founded in 1896). She was the director of the NACW's Mothers' Club in Brooklyn and was part of the female auxiliary of the radical Niagara Movement in 1905 and 1906. She also participated in the work of the Committee for Improving Industrial Conditions of Negroes in New York City (founded in 1906), which in 1911 merged with two other social reform groups to become the National Urban League.

Morton-Jones fought to win the vote for all women and fought to protect the right to vote of all black Americans. She rejected the notion that black women had no interest in voting. She assisted in conducting voter education programs, noted instances of race discrimination at the polls, and testified before congressional investigatory committees. Like many other black clubwomen of the Progressive Era, Morton-Jones drew on the tradition of self-help in the black community in her tenure as president of the Brooklyn Equal Suffrage League.

Morton-Jones was elected to the **National Association for the Advancement of Colored People** (NAACP) Board of Directors in 1913 and worked on the executive committee until 1925. Mary White Ovington, a white social reformer and one of the founders of the NAACP, in her 1947 autobiography *The Walls Came Tumbling Down*, reminisced about a typical 1917 board meeting in which Morton-Jones was the only "colored woman."

Morton-Jones was not the only woman of color to have membership in the interracial Cosmopolitan Club, however. This social and political group of New York City and Brooklyn reformers met regularly to discuss racism, civil rights, and reform stratagems. Morton-Jones, Ovington, *Independent* editor Hamilton Holt, prominent socialist John Spargo, and the *Evening Post*'s Oswald Garrison Villard were among the members of this club. Both black and white reformers active in groups such as the NAACP and the Urban League attended its meetings. Morton-Jones also held membership in the Association for the Protection of Colored Women, and volunteered for the "Phillis Wheatley" chapters of the **Young Women's Christian Association** (YWCA).

Morton-Jones is at once an outstanding and a typical example of those black professionals and clubwomen who sought to "uplift" their communities by working within both black and interracial protest groups to combat racism and protect civil rights. An Episcopalian and a Republican, Morton-Jones died in 1943.

THEA ARNOLD

K

Kneeland, Francis M. (b. c. 1873)

Francis M. Kneeland was one of the pioneer black women physicians to graduate from Meharry Medical College in Nashville, Tennessee. Kneeland was part of the first generation of black women doctors who practiced in the United States in the late nineteenth and early twentieth centuries. However, only sketchy information exists about their experiences. The first black women physicians not only were the first women of their race to practice medicine, but also were among the first female physicians in the country.

Born in Tennessee c. 1873, Francis Kneeland lost her parents at an early age. Where or exactly when she was born, when she was orphaned, or the names of her parents—all these are unknown. She raised her younger siblings and educated them and herself. She graduated from Meharry, one of the foremost training institutions of black physicians in the country, with honors in 1898.

A few years earlier, in 1893, Dr. Georgiana Patton and Dr. Annie D. Gregg had become the first women to receive medical degrees from Meharry. Dr. Patton went on to become the first black woman to be licensed to practice surgery and medicine in Tennessee. She located in Memphis, becoming the city's first black woman physician. Dr. Patton established a large and successful practice, and she remained in the city until her death in 1900 at the age of thirty-six.

Dr. Francis Kneeland followed closely on the trail blazed by Patton, and by 1907–08 her name appears in the Memphis directory as Dr. Francis M. Kneeland, physician and surgeon, with an office at 168 Beale Avenue. In addition to her private practice, Dr. Kneeland was closely associated with the University of West Tennessee in Memphis. The university was a medical school (founded by Miles V. Lynk in 1901) that provided training for minorities for sixteen years. Although the school was established as an institution of higher learning for black Americans, other minorities received training, and so, for instance, six Japanese students graduated with the class of 1923. The university had conferred 216 medical degrees by 1924. Dr. Kneeland served as the head instructor of the nursing program.

She was an excellent lecturer, and was known for her involvement in associations that worked for the uplift and improvement of black women. Because she was the only black woman physician in the city, she was seen as an important role model who demonstrated what women with character could achieve professionally. She was the favored physician of hundreds of women in the city, and she seems to have successfully combined a private practice with teaching, nurses' training, and public service work.

In addition, Dr. Kneeland made a good business decision when she located her office on Beale Street, important not only as the birthplace of the blues, but also as a uniquely diverse and multiethnic area of the city where black and white, European and Asian, urban and rural, and wealthy and poor people all lived and worked. By 1908, over forty black doctors in Memphis had their offices on or near Beale Street. Most were, like Dr. Kneeland, graduates of Meharry who had settled in Memphis because its black population (about 52,500, in 1910) needed access to, and could pay for, medical care. Black physicians formed the upper crust of the black community. Evidently Dr. Kneeland was able to benefit from these opportunities, for she purchased her own home in one of the more prosperous sections of the city. However, for reasons unknown, Dr. Kneeland left Memphis (it is not known exactly when) to reside in Chicago with relatives.

EARNESTINE JENKINS

L

Lacks, Henrietta (1920?–1951)

She was a working-class housewife and mother of five, respectable, lovely, and quietly religious. She never went to college, never studied science, and died of cancer at the age of 31. Yet she has played a crucial role in modern science, and medical researchers who have never heard her name are indebted to her for their successes.

Henrietta Lacks walked into medical history one winter day in the early 1950s, when she arrived at Johns Hopkins Hospital. She was soon diagnosed with cervical cancer. The cancer grew rapidly, and she died ten months later. Her husband, David Lacks, Sr., gave permission for an autopsy but no other medical procedure. The family had no idea that anything else was in store.

One of the researchers who worked on Lacks' case was Dr. George Gey, a leader in cancer tissue culture. In order to study cancer—or any other cell disease—there must be cells to study. The problem is that human cells can survive only for a short time out of the body, which makes them useless for most experiments. Working with Lacks' cells, Gey noticed something remarkable. Unlike ordinary human cells, they did not die in the laboratory. They reproduced aggressively and thrived under laboratory conditions.

While Henrietta Lacks died in 1951, her cells—now known as HeLa cells—have continued to live and reproduce. Because of this strange immortality, they became the basis of experiments around the world.

At first the spread was accidental. Cancer cells are able to invade other tissue and leave their imprint on other cells' chromosomes. The HeLa cells invaded other tissue samples at Johns Hopkins. Since tissue samples are often exchanged at research laboratories around the world, HeLa cells began to spread.

HeLa cells became the basis of cell-line culture, a medical specialty that made Gey famous. However, Lacks' family was not asked if the cells could be used. They were not even notified until decades after her death.

HeLa cells are a basic part of a modern medical research laboratory. They have been instrumental in the study of cancer, viruses, and other diseases. They were used to develop the polio vaccine. Henrietta Lacks' cells are used to study the effects on health of nutrition, pollution, or environmental factors. They are used to study the dangerous side-effects of X-rays, and the bases of congenital diseases. In short, Lacks' cells are the basic reference cell used in laboratories all around the world. As one researcher has put it: "There isn't a cancer research laboratory anywhere that hasn't used HeLa cells."

As famous as HeLa cells are, few of the researchers who depend on Henrietta Lack's cells know her name. The few times when she is mentioned in medical texts she is usually listed as Helen Lane or Helen Larson. Even so, Henrietta's strange immortality has earned her a certain cult status among young researchers. Graffiti on the wall of one research facility proclaims: "Helen Lane Lives!"

ANDRA MEDEA

Lattimer, Agnes D. (1928–)

"Many things we need can wait," Agnes Lattimer once observed, but "the children cannot." An abiding concern for the welfare of children motivated Lattimer to become a pediatrician, to work tirelessly for systems of preventative medicine for children, and, ultimately, because of her talents and efforts, to become the medical director of Cook County Hospital, one of the nation's largest public hospitals.

Agnes Lattimer was born on May 13, 1928, in Memphis, Tennessee. Her father, who worked in the insurance industry, and her mother, Hortense, had four other children as well. Agnes' mother recalled that as early as age ten, her daughter had expressed a firm desire to become a doctor, a pilot, and a pianist—all of which she became. Lattimer graduated magna cum laude from Fisk University in 1949 with a B.S. in biology. Heading north to Chicago, she entered the Chicago Medical School, where she earned her M.D. in 1954. Over the next four years, she did her internship and residency in pediatric medicine at Cook County Hospital. In 1960, she became a fellow of the American Board of Pediatrics.

In addition to a demanding practice in pediatric medicine, Lattimer also embarked on a teaching career at both the University of Illinois School of Public Health and the

With her appointment as medical director of Cook County Hospital in Chicago, Illinois, one of the nation's largest public hospitals, Agnes D. Lattimer became the only black woman in the United States to hold the top medical post in a major hospital in a major city. (COOK COUNTY HOSPITAL)

University of Chicago School of Medicine. She still holds a full professorship in the University of Chicago's Department of Pediatrics.

Over the course of her career, Lattimer also has become more and more committed to the providing of health care for poor people. Throughout her years as a practicing physician and as an administrator, Lattimer has insisted that medical personnel treat all patients with respect and dignity, regardless of their ability to pay: "People often refer to care for the poor as 'free care,' but too often we exact the most significant coin . . . from these patients . . . their self-respect."

After serving as associate director of ambulatory care and as director of the Fantus Health Center, both at Cook County Hospital, Lattimer was appointed temporary medical director of the hospital in February 1986; in March 1986, when that appointment became permanent, Lattimer became the only black woman in the country to hold the top medical post in a major hospital in a major city. As medical director she oversees the activities of 350 doctors and 475 interns and residents in the 1,200-bed facility. Her role, she has said, is that of problem-solver: "There is a constant barrage of problems that occur at a hospital, and the medical director is the one who develops options and plots a course of action."

Agnes Lattimer's work schedule leaves little time for her family, which includes a grown son, Bernard Goss, or for her two favorite hobbies, flying and bridge, but she says she would have it no other way. "It's a very demanding job. . . . It's what I wanted . . . and I like it."

CHRISTINE A. LUNARDINI

Laurie, Eunice Rivers (1899–1986)

In 1958, public health nurse Eunice Rivers Laurie received the U.S. Department of Health, Education and Welfare's (HEW) highest honor, the Oveta Culp Hobby Award, for her "notable service covering twenty-five years, during which through selfless devotion and skillful human rela-

tions she has sustained the interest and cooperation of the subjects of a venereal disease control program in Macon County, Alabama." Fourteen years later, media coverage revealed what is often considered to be this country's most heinous medical experiment: Nurse Rivers, as she was known, had been crucial in sustaining a forty-year study by the U.S. Public Health Service of late-stage syphilis in nearly 400 black men that kept the men ignorant of their disease while denying them treatment. Her role in the "Tuskegee Experiment" is still debated by the public, media, and scholars alike, even becoming the subject of an often-produced play and of television documentaries.

Eunice Verdell Rivers was born on November 12, 1899, in Early County, Georgia, the oldest child of three in the family of Albert and Henrietta Rivers. Rivers' mother died when she was fifteen, and her father gained a modicum of independence by working a small farm while he held on to his job in a sawmill. Eunice Rivers remembers that after her father was wrongly accused of aiding in the escape of a black man wanted for the murder of a white policeman, a Ku Klux Klan member shot a bullet into their home. To save the family, Albert Rivers moved them into a rented house while he protected their home.

Eunice Rivers first went to a school under the tutelage of a cousin in Fort Gaines, Georgia, and then to a mission boarding school in Thomasville. When Albert Rivers discovered that the mission school had only white teachers in the upper grades, he pulled his daughter out (one year shy of high school graduation) and sent her to the Tuskegee Institute in Alabama in 1918.

Eunice Rivers spent her first year at Tuskegee learning handicrafts, in keeping with the school's philosophy of vocational education. In response to her father's urging, she switched to nursing. Graduating from Tuskegee Institute in 1922, she did some private nursing, and then was hired to travel with Tuskegee's Moveable School, a truck that carried an agricultural extension agent, a home demonstration agent, a public health nurse, and their equipment into Alabama's countryside.

Rivers focused primarily on the health needs of black women and children, teaching basic health education, simple sanitation methods, and well-child care. She also demonstrated cleanliness techniques to Alabama's extensive network of granny midwives. At the time, she was one of only four black public health nurses in the entire state. She also worked for the state's Bureau of Vital Statistics, devising techniques whereby midwives would report births accurately.

For many, Rivers' great skill was her nonjudgmental understanding of the medical beliefs of rural black people and her support for their dignity and individual needs in medical encounters. By 1931, the state had cut its work force and Rivers had lost her position. She was then hired as a night supervisor at Tuskegee Institute's Andrews Hospital.

Eight months and many sleepless nights later, she was offered a half-time day position: scientific assistant for the Public Health Service's study formally called "Untreated Syphilis in the Male Negro." Rivers' job for the next forty years was to help in finding men for the study, following up on their conditions, assisting in their examinations, gaining agreement from their families for autopsies, and modifying the primarily white physicians' behaviors toward their "subjects." Nurse Rivers was central to securing the compliance of the men to painful spinal taps and diagnostic procedures, providing rubs and aspirin— and ensuring that they did not receive treatment for their disease.

When the story of the experiment broke on the Associated Press wire on July 26, 1972, it caused an uproar across the country. The issues of racism, genocidal medicine, paternalism gone awry, and the health care system's notorious willingness to use poor and illiterate people for experimentation without their informed consent were debated. Senator Edward Kennedy convened hearings in the U.S. Senate, an HEW investigation condemned the study, the institutions and medical groups involved offered varying justifications, and a class-action civil suit filed by prominent civil rights attorney Fred Gray ended in a $10 million out-of-court settlement for survivors and their families. Nurse Rivers never testified before the Senate hearings, nor was she named in the suit.

Eunice Rivers spent almost all of her adult life in Tuskegee, Alabama, turning down an opportunity to work in a New York City hospital in 1932. She spent half of her time in maternal and child health clinics at the Andrews Hospital. In 1952, she married Julius Laurie, an orderly at the hospital. She was also active in the Red Cross and at the Greater St. Mark Missionary Baptist Church in Tuskegee. Numerous awards testified to her nursing skills. Eunice Rivers died in Tuskegee on August 28, 1986.

Differing interpretations exist of the reasons why Eunice Rivers participated in the syphilis research for so long. For some, she is the prototypical naive nurse deferring to male physicians' authority, rationalizing the racism because of her status in the black community. Others suggest that she was less deferential, and was moved by her ability to provide some medical attention to a community that usually received none at all. For still others, her story symbolizes the constraints exerted in all moral decision making. More complex interpretations will have to give greater weight to her dignity, her power over the white physicians who needed her, the context of the black health movement of the early twentieth century, and her own understanding of her efforts.

SUSAN M. REVERBY

Logan, Myra Adele (1908–1977)

"If you're interested in any field of humanity," physician Myra Logan said of her chosen profession, "you can't miss if you go into medicine." She followed in the family tradition: her mother, an aunt, and a sister were deeply involved with health issues, and a brother and a brother-in-law were physicians.

Myra Adele Logan was born in 1908 in Tuskegee, Alabama, the eighth child of Warren and Adella Hunt Logan. She completed her early education at Tuskegee, then obtained a bachelor's degree at Atlanta University in 1929.

She moved to New York City and earned a master's degree from Columbia University, working as well with the Young Men's Christian Association (YMCA). Logan then attended and graduated from the school of medicine of New York's Flower Fifth Avenue Hospital. She spent most of her professional career at Harlem Hospital. Her work in developing antibiotics, and her achievements in open-heart surgery, brought her great respect in the medical community. She had a private practice and belonged to a joint medical insurance group as well. She worked with both Planned Parenthood and the **National Association for the Advancement of Colored People** (NAACP), was published in numerous medical journals, and was one of the first black females to be elected to the American College of Physicians and Surgeons.

Logan had little time to play, but she was nonetheless a skilled classical pianist. In 1943, she married painter Charles Alston; the couple had no children. She died of lung cancer in 1977.

ADELE LOGAN ALEXANDER

M

Mahoney, Carolyn R. (1946–)

Carolyn Mahoney's creative talents have been employed since 1989 as the first mathematician on the faculty of a new college, California State University at San Marcos. Known as an effective teacher, she was invited by the Committee on Student Chapters of the Mathematical Association of America (MAA) to speak about "Contemporary Problems in Graph Theory" at the national MAA meeting in Baltimore in January 1992. She has given talks on both mathematical research (combinatorics, graph theory, and matroids) and pedagogy throughout the United States and the People's Republic of China.

Carolyn Mahoney was born in Memphis, Tennessee, on December 22, 1946, to Stephen and Myrtle Boone. In 1970, she received her B.S. in mathematics from Siena College in Memphis. Her M.S. and Ph.D. in mathematics were awarded by Ohio State University in 1972 and 1983, respectively. She has taught at Denison University in Granville, Ohio (1984–89), and Ohio State University (1987–89). She and her husband Charles have three daughters.

She is coordinator of the Young Scholars Program, a year-round, comprehensive, pre-college program for low-income Appalachian, Hispanic, and black students in Ohio. She directed a program to improve the achievement of black students in mathematics at four Ohio liberal arts schools. From 1986 to 1989, she was a member of the test development committee of the College Board. She has served on many boards and prestigious committees, contributed to numerous policy-setting documents, won several grants, and given dozens of invited talks. On March 20, 1989, Carolyn Mahoney was inducted into the Ohio Women's Hall of Fame.

PATRICIA CLARK KENSCHAFT

Mahoney, Mary Eliza (1845–1926)

The first trained black nurse in the United States, Mary Eliza Mahoney was born in Dorchester, Massachusetts, on May 7, 1845, to Charles and Mary Jane Stewart Mahoney. On August 1, 1879, she completed a sixteen-month diploma program in nursing at the New England Hospital for Women and Children in Boston, at a time when the institution's charter stipulated that each class include only one black student and one Jewish student.

Mahoney registered with the Nurses Directory at the Massachusetts Medical Library in Boston upon receipt of her diploma. Like the vast majority of new nurses, she first entered private-duty nursing. Not until after World War II would the majority of nurses secure staff employment in hospitals, and black nurses would wait even longer for hospital staff appointments.

Mahoney was able to secure membership in the Nurses Associated Alumnae of the United States and Canada, organized in 1896 and later renamed the American Nurses Association (ANA). At the turn of the century, few black nurses were allowed to become members of the ANA, because nurses were required to become members of state nursing associations before they were granted membership in the national organization, and Southern associations refused to admit black women.

After black nurses organized their own organization, the **National Association of Colored Graduate Nurses** (NACGN), in 1908, Mahoney delivered the welcoming address at its first convention in Boston in August 1909. The members honored Mahoney in 1911 by awarding her life membership in the NACGN, and electing her national chaplain, a position that bore the responsibility for the induction of new officers.

In 1911, Mahoney became supervisor of the Howard Orphan Asylum for black children in Kings Park, Long Island. She retired in 1922, but continued to participate in and observe the activities of the NACGN until her death on January 4, 1926.

As a lasting tribute, the NACGN established in 1936 an award in her name to honor distinguished black nurses. When the NACGN merged with the ANA in 1951, the practice of giving the Mary Mahoney Award was preserved. In 1976, she was named to the Nursing Hall of Fame.

DARLENE CLARK HINE

McCarroll, Ernest Mae (1898–1990)

Ernest Mae McCarroll was the first black physician permitted to practice at Newark City Hospital in 1946, in an era when, as she said, "Negro doctors had no other choice than to leave their patients at the front door."

Born in Birmingham, Alabama, on November 29, 1898, McCarroll earned a B.A. from Talladega College in 1917 and entered medical school at the Woman's Medical College of Pennsylvania in 1919. She graduated in 1925, interned at Kansas City General Hospital No. 2, and entered general practice in Philadelphia.

In 1929, she moved to Newark, New Jersey, where she established a private practice and pioneered in the fight against sexually transmitted diseases. In that year she also married Leroy Baxter, a dentist. Ten years later they were divorced. McCarroll had two subsequent marriages (1958, 1983).

During the 1930s, McCarroll worked as a clinic physician with the Newark Department of Health, lecturing about hygiene and venereal diseases to women throughout the city.

She received her M.S. in public health from Columbia University in 1939, and did postgraduate work at the Harvard University School of Public Health. McCarroll was a member of the board of trustees of the National Medical Association (NMA) 1949–55 and 1963–73. She was named First Lady of the NMA for her work, and the New Jersey Medical Society named her its first General Practitioner of the Year in 1955.

She retired in 1973 and died in a Florida nursing home on February 20, 1990.

SUSAN SHIFRIN

N

Nash, Helen E. (1921–)

"Sell a house and send her to medical school," said Helen Nash's grandfather on his deathbed in 1941. A successful Atlanta property owner, he knew that one of his assets would be enough to support her for the first year. Though her father was a physician, he was skeptical of his daughter's commitment to medicine.

As it turned out, supporting Helen Nash's medical education proved to be a wise investment with a rich return. In 1989, Dr. Helen Nash celebrated her fortieth anniversary in practice. During those years, she became a distinguished pediatrician and child advocate. Now Clinical Professor of Pediatrics at the Washington University School of Medicine, in 1949 she was the only woman among the first four black doctors to integrate the medical staff there.

Helen Nash was born on August 8, 1921. She grew up in a prosperous family where education and culture were highly valued. Her father was Homer Erwin Nash, M.D., and her mother was Marie Graves Nash, a music teacher. A graduate of **Spelman College** in her native Atlanta, and of Meharry Medical College in Nashville, Helen Nash performed well academically. Despite harsh discrimination against black Americans and women in medicine, she was determined to become a physician, and her upbringing and education had given her the self-confidence she would need to succeed.

In 1945, she arrived in St. Louis to take a rotating internship at Homer G. Phillips Hospital, one of the few institutions in the country then offering postgraduate training to minority physicians. Opened in 1937 as a segregated hospital to serve the black community, "Homer G." (as it was known) was famous for giving young doctors superb clinical experience. Dr. Nash worked on twelve services during her internship year, and took three additional years of residency training in pediatrics. There she met Dr. Park J. White, the senior supervising pediatrician from the Washington University School of Medicine. Unlike many colleagues at this time, he felt a deep commitment to improving medical care for black children. Concerned about the rate of black infant mortality in 1924, when he surveyed the problem in St. Louis, White saw a great need for well-trained black physicians and immediately recognized Helen Nash's promise. He encouraged her to become board-certified, and she passed the examination without difficulty.

Despite differences in age, race, and gender, an extraordinary collaboration developed between these two pediatricians. By 1947, they had helped to increase the pressure necessary to integrate St. Louis Children's Hospital, the city's major pediatric teaching institution. They pressed successfully for improved standards of care and hygiene at Homer Phillips Hospital, where newborns were still sleeping in partitioned

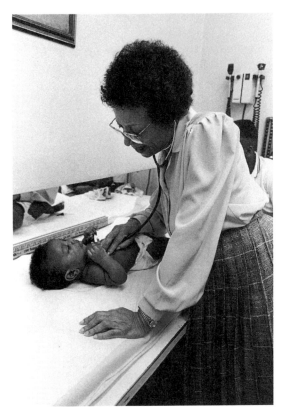

A distinguished physician and child advocate, Helen Nash revolutionized conditions at St. Louis Children's Hospital. (TOM HEINE)

group spaces, rather than in individual bassinets.

Supported by funds from the U.S. Children's Bureau, Dr. White and Dr. Nash raised health standards and lowered mortality rates. The mean details of segregation infuriated Dr. Nash. Sick black children received no ice cream, and bananas only on rare occasions, while these consoling items routinely were given to other pediatric patients at City Hospital No. 1. Dr. Nash took pride in confronting bureaucrats and demanding that they change this policy. By 1949, as a result of her work with Dr. White, the premature babies' death rate had dropped from 80 percent to 16 percent.

Infant mortality remains a major concern for Helen Nash today. She is indignant that infants in the United States die more often than children in twenty-two other nations, with black babies dying at twice the rate of others—a ratio that has not changed since her mentor, Dr. White, surveyed the problem in 1924. Over her long career, Dr. Nash has built both a thriving practice and an outstanding reputation as a child advocate. Even while many local physicians were moving to the suburbs, she continued to maintain a busy office in downtown St. Louis, where she now treats her third generation of patients. Some families who have moved to outlying areas bring their youngsters back to her for care.

Dr. Nash's bonds with children are all-inclusive; her concerns reach well beyond the confines of private practice. As a 1976 honor citation from the St. Louis Medical Society states: "She has given of her time and herself unstintingly throughout her career in improving the health of all children regardless of socioeconomic or ethnic status." In 1974, she spent six weeks developing rural health clinics in the Philippines because, as she said in an interview: "I had always been envious of Peace Corps volunteers and wanted to see if I could do something like that myself."

Dr. Nash has a long record of commitment to providing family planning services for the black community, and she sees no conflict between this and her role as a pediatrician. Indeed, she feels that she has a special responsibility to make sure that children are born to parents ready to nurture them. Her pediatric practice extends beyond adolescence, when necessary, and includes the provision of contraceptive counseling because, as she says, "By the time an adolescent is pregnant, it's already too late."

She calls herself a "rabid feminist," and believes that women must learn to speak up for themselves. She has been a powerful role model for many; indeed, an unusual number of former women patients have become physicians. Other former patients have achieved success in various fields, among them Harry Hampton, the well-known producer of *Eyes on the Prize,* a documentary film history of the civil rights movement. At her fortieth anniversary celebration, Hampton said: "Helen's life is a broad, rich quilt. She is a pioneer for both her race and her gender. . . . Our chief want in life is to find someone who can help us to do what we can—Helen is that for many. . . . She is a long-distance runner, who connects the now to then and to what will be."

In addition to her responsibilities at the Washington University School of Medicine, Helen Nash holds an Honor Membership in the St. Louis Medical Society, is a member of the American Medical Association, the Missouri State Medical Association, and the St. Louis Pediatric Society. She is a trustee of the St. Louis Symphony and of the Missouri Botanical Gardens. In 1992, she also received two honorary degrees: a doctor of humane letters from Webster University, and a doctor of humane letters from the University of Missouri in St. Louis.

MARION HUNT

National Association of Colored Graduate Nurses

At the end of the nineteenth century, the status of black nurses was appalling. Throughout the United States they were denied adequate training. They were kept out of most hospital and private-duty nursing. When they found employment, they were paid significantly lower wages than white nurses. They were not allowed to serve as nurses in the armed forces. Their inferior status in the profession was reinforced by separate state board examinations and exclusion from nursing organizations. Worst of all, they had to stand by helplessly as their own people were denied health care that they themselves could have provided.

On August 25, 1908, a group of fifty-two black graduate nurses met at St. Mark's Methodist Church in New York City to try to change these conditions. The force behind the gathering was **Martha Franklin,** from New Haven, Connecticut. She had recently surveyed hundreds of black nurses about their professional situations, and the results had made her decide that they must take matters into their own hands. Franklin was elected president of the organization at that first meeting, and the major issues were aired. When the women left, they had three goals: to advance the standards and best interests of trained nurses, to break down discrimination in the nursing profession, and to develop leadership within the ranks of black nurses. They were also fiercely determined to improve health care for black patients.

In the years that followed, the National Association of Colored Graduate Nurses

(NACGN) battled on all fronts. In 1909, the organization set out to destroy the practice of having separate state boards of nursing. One member, Ludie A. Andrews, instituted legal proceedings against the state of Georgia and fought for the next ten years for the right to sit for the same professional licensing examination as her white peers. In 1917, the organization created a national registry of black graduate nurses to help its members find employment, especially private-duty employment. In 1920, it began a campaign to improve black-operated nursing schools.

In 1934, the NACGN established a national headquarters and hired a nurse executive secretary, **Mabel Keaton Staupers.** Two years later, three black schools of nursing were accredited by the New York State Board of Nurse Examiners. In the same year, a public health nursing program for graduate black nurses was established at St. Phillip Hospital in Richmond, Virginia.

In the years that followed, the NACGN worked for legislation that would improve the lot of its members and the black community as a whole. In 1943, it supported an amendment to the Bolton Bill that would create the Cadet Nurse Corps, ensuring that black nursing students would be able to join the corps. By the war's end, more than 2,000 black students had participated. The organization also worked with the army, pressuring it to drop its restrictions against black nurses. As a result, more than 500 black nurses served in the army in World War II. The group was less successful in its dealings with the navy, in which only four black nurses served.

The final obstacle to full participation in professional nursing was the American Nurses Association (ANA). By 1949, through the efforts of the NACGN, only nine states and the District of Columbia still barred black nurses from their local ANA chapters, and provisions had been made for individuals to bypass those chapters and join the ANA directly.

On January 25, 1951, the board of directors of the National Association of Colored Graduate Nurses, having decided that its job was done, voted itself out of existence.

MARIE MOSLEY

National Negro Health Week

The dismal state of black health care in the United States spawned a grass-roots black health movement that began largely as a local effort by black women's groups. Midwives, mothers, nurses, teachers, and sororities organized and participated in activities that provided health services and information to the community. "From 1890 to 1920 the health activities of organized women's clubs laid the foundation for the black health movement."

Slavery was a flagrant violation of fundamental human rights, one of which was the right to health and an adequate health care system. Therefore, African Americans, in direct response to racism and segregation, built hospitals and medical schools to address black health care needs. **Howard University** and Meharry Medical College were among the first fourteen black medical schools to be founded in the United States.

The health care deficits established during the time of slavery continued well into the twentieth century. "For example, in

1900 the black death rate was 25 per 1,000 compared to 17 per 1,000 in whites. Although the black rate dropped in 1930 to 14 per 1,000, it was still considerably higher than the white rate of 10."

In 1915, Booker Taliaferro Washington founded National Negro Health Week (NNHW) in an effort to increase the awareness and improve the health status of African Americans. This observance brought national attention to the black health care crisis, and it was the catalyst for the National Negro Health Movement, officially launched in 1932.

The Negro Organization Society of Virginia also played a major role in providing the foundation for the National Negro Health Movement. Under the direction of Robert Russa Moton in 1912, this organization started day-long campaigns to clean up the farms and neighborhoods in Virginia. With the support of the Virginia Board of Health, the campaign expanded to a week.

In 1914, Monroe Nathan Work, a sociologist at Tuskegee Institute, provided an alarming statistical analysis of black Americans' health in the South. His calculations indicated that nearly half of all black deaths were premature and could have been prevented. These data, combined with the activity of local health activists, inspired Booker T. Washington to envision a national health movement. In 1915, he initiated a Health Improvement Week at Tuskegee Institute. This became National Negro Health Week (NNHW), to promote health and disease prevention among African Americans. Sixteen states participated during the first year. Lectures at schools and churches, distribution of health pamphlets, and special cleanup services took

place across the country. After Washington died on November 14, 1915, plans for a National Negro Health Week in 1916 did not materialize. In 1917, however, under the leadership of Tuskegee faculty members Moton and Work, Washington's efforts were renewed and the institutionalization of NNHW began.

They decided to honor Booker T. Washington as founder of the movement by celebrating National Negro Health Week during the first week in April, to commemorate his birth on April 5. They also wanted to expand the week into a year-round program. Health leaders concluded that the best way to do this was to get the U.S. Public Health Service (USPHS) to take over NNHW.

In 1932, NNHW came under the purview of the USPHS, and this branch of the government became the center for all activity concerning black health issues. The name "National Negro Health Movement" was coined, and the USPHS opened the Office of Negro Health Work under the direction of Dr. Roscoe C. Brown. Activities sparked by NNHW survived well into the 1940s, and were supported by minority and nonminority associations and public health departments. Various health education and special clinical services were sponsored nationwide. During this time, Dr. Brown kept records of participation throughout the country. He reported that the number of people reached through NNHW had increased from 500,000 in 1933 to 5,000,000 in 1942. These figures suggest that it was indeed a mass movement.

From 1932 to 1950, a quarterly newsletter chronicling the movement, the *National Negro Health News,* was published. In

1950, the USPHS declared the end of the black health program and closed the NNHW office. Although the health status of African Americans had improved sig- nificantly, a two-tiered health care system remained, one for white Americans and one for black Americans.

LESA WALDEN

O

Osborne, Estelle Massey (1901–1981)

Estelle Massey Osborne devoted her life to nursing—as a practitioner and as an advocate for improved training and better job opportunities for black nurses.

Estelle Massey was born on May 3, 1901, in Palestine, Texas, eighth of the eleven children of Hall and Bettye Estelle Massey, a remarkable couple with strong opinions about childrearing. The Massey children raised and sold vegetables in order to gain spending money. The Massey daughters were not allowed to work for white employers, because their mother did not want them to be exposed to racism. The Masseys brought up their children to be strong, confident, and proud.

Estelle Massey kept alive her parents' dreams for her by attending Prairie View State College. After graduation, she taught, became a nurse, and then taught nursing. At that point, she decided that she needed more education.

While attending Teachers College, Columbia University, in New York, Massey taught at Lincoln Hospital School for Nurses in the Bronx. Later she was hired by Harlem Hospital School of Nursing, becoming the first black nursing instructor there. After receiving her bachelor's degree from Columbia in 1931, she became the first educational director of nursing at Freedmen's Hospital School of Nursing (now **Howard University** College of Nursing). Her goal while at Freedmen's was to provide black student nurses with the same quality of education that white students were receiving at the best nursing schools, but Osborne had another goal as well. She wanted to change the quality of education for black nurses across the country.

Working through the **National Association of Colored Graduate Nurses (NACGN)**, as well as on her own, Osborne

A courageous advocate for black nurses, Estelle Massey Osborne fought to lift the color ban in the Army and Navy Nurse Corps. (MOORLAND-SPINGARN)

organized conferences, gave seminars, and conducted workshops all over the country. For five years, she was president of the NACGN.

In 1936, Osborne became the first black director of nursing at City Hospital No. 2 (now the Homer G. Phillips Hospital Training School). In 1943, she served as a consultant to the National Nursing Council for War Service. As the first black consultant on the staff of any national nursing organization, she helped to increase the number of white nurses' training schools admitting black students from fourteen to thirty-eight in just two years. She also fought to lift the color ban on black nurses attempting to enlist in the Army and Navy Nurse Corps and, with the army, was successful.

In 1946, she received her master's degree and became the first black member of the nursing faculty at New York University in New York City. This position brought Osborne a great deal of visibility and prestige and allowed her to make even greater strides in her fight for the advancement of black nurses. In 1948, she won a position on the board of directors of the American Nurses Association.

In the years that followed, Osborne served in an executive position with most of the important nursing organizations in the country. When she retired in 1967, she was associate general director of the National League for Nursing. Estelle Massey Osborne died in 1981.

MARIE MOSLEY

P

Petioni, Muriel Marjorie (1914–)

Soon after Muriel Petioni, M.D., opened her medical practice in Harlem in 1950, she learned the necessity of integrating medical treatment with the social and economic realities that impacted upon her patients. Many could not afford the $2 or $3 she charged for an office visit or house call, and so they sometimes paid her with food. Popular because of her holistic approach to treatment, Dr. Petioni worked as New York City Department of Health School Physician between 1950 and 1980. In her practice at 114 W. 131 Street she pioneered in the successful treatment of drug addiction, for which she was honored by the city of New York in 1983. She remains an activist for health care delivery and is affiliated with many health-related and community institutions.

Petioni has been concerned throughout her career with women's issues, and women's advancement in the male-dominated medical profession. In 1974, she started one of the first organizations of black women doctors, the New York-area **Susan Smith McKinney Steward** Medical Society, named for the prominent nineteenth-century Brooklyn physician. She continued as its first president until 1984. In 1977, Dr. Petioni organized black women physicians nationally in Medical Women of the National Medical Association. It was the first female physicians' group to be officially admitted as a component of the Black National Medical Association formed in 1985.

Muriel Marjorie Petioni was born in Port of Spain, Trinidad, on January 1, 1914, the daughter of Rose Alling, a de-

A pioneer in the successful treatment of drug addiction, Muriel Petioni started one of the first organizations of black women doctors, the New York-area Susan Smith McKinney Steward Medical Society, named for the well-known nineteenth-century physician.

111

partment store clerk, and Charles Augustin Petioni, a newspaper reporter. The family immigrated to New York City when Muriel was five. Her father became a prominent Harlem physician, activist, and champion of Caribbean independence. She attended public schools 68, 136, and Wadleigh High School. After two years at New York University she entered an accelerated program at **Howard University,** one of two black medical schools in Washington, D.C., and graduated with a B.S. in 1934 and an M.D. in 1937.

In 1939, she completed her internship at Harlem Hospital, one of the few hospitals admitting black interns to its training program, and then did her residency at the black-operated Homer Phillips Hospital in St. Louis, Missouri. In 1942, she married Mallalieu S. Woolfolk, a lawyer. They have one son, Charles M. Woolfolk, a New York businessman.

Before returning to New York City in 1950, Dr. Petioni practiced as a college physician at several black institutions. In 1951, after her father's death, she established a family practice in her father's office in Harlem, where she continued to practice until her retirement in 1990.

In some, ways Dr. Petioni's career is characteristic of black women physicians of her generation, whose approach to medical practice brought them into direct contact with community and family concerns. Typically excluded from surgical specialties, these medical women were the organizers within local and national medical societies, and more often than their male colleagues they were leaders in the larger community. Dr. Petioni's initiation of formal organization among black women physicians in the 1970s reflected growing feminist concerns among black professional women, who were encouraged by their expanding numbers and the need to organize the support they could receive only from other women.

IRMA WATKINS-OWENS

S

Sanders, Maude (1903–1995)

Teacher, physician, and crusader for medical justice, Maude Sanders was born in New Orleans, Louisiana, in 1903 to John E. and Sophronia Sanders. She was the youngest of ten children. Her father was born in Natchez, Mississippi, in 1860. It is speculated that he was the son of a white slave master. Sanders remembers her father as a carpenter who built his own house and worked for a shipbuilding company in New Orleans. In an interview, Sanders said that her father was a brilliant man who knew how many nails were required to build a warmer house and who could calculate the amount of wallpaper required to paper a house as efficiently as a college graduate, although he had only a grade school education. While working with her father, Sanders learned to hammer a nail "as efficiently as any man."

Her mother Sophronia was born in Natchez, Mississippi, in 1871. She did not finish school, but had enough education to teach grade school. She also took in laundry to help meet the family's economic needs. Sanders' mother taught her how to sew, and both parents taught their children the value of education.

Maude Sanders' formal education began at age seven, when she entered Miro School, the first school for black students to be built in her district. Prior to the construction of Miro, black children had to walk nine miles to school. Maude entered the school in 1910 and graduated in 1918. By the time of her graduation from elementary school, New Orleans had built one high school for the all black school-children in the city. Sanders enrolled in the McDonough High School and graduated in 1922.

Like most of her peers, Sanders decided to take a job teaching. She found work in Convent, Louisiana, a small rural area where she taught for two years. She boarded with a mulatto family whose young daughter told Sanders that she was too black to take a bath in the same tin wash tub used by the family. Unhappy that the children went to school only for two months of the year and worked on farms the other ten, Sanders left Convent in 1924 and returned to New Orleans.

She enrolled at Xavier, a black Roman Catholic college, and entered the two-year teaching program because teaching seemed to be the only career open to black women other than working in someone's kitchen. There were few teaching jobs, however, because there were only a few schools for black children, and few black children were able to attend school because they had to work.

When she graduated, Sanders was unable to find a teaching job because the public schools would not hire teachers trained in Catholic schools. So, she resigned herself to substitute teaching and making suits in a tailor shop owned by a

German Jew who had hired her over a white applicant because she was more diligent and wanted to learn how to make perfect buttonholes on men's suits. The sewing skills her mother had taught her turned out to be very useful in that job.

In 1928, after working in the tailor shop for a year, Sanders, now twenty-five, married a man with an eighth-grade education. Most black men at the time did not have the opportunity to get an education, because they had to work. Unfortunately, her husband thought of himself as inferior to her, and so they were divorced after a few years.

Maude Sanders' chance to pursue a career in medicine came shortly after her divorce, when her two sisters, Naomi, a teacher, and Lillian, a beautician, after consulting with one of Maude's former teachers, suggested that she study medicine. Since childhood, Sanders had been interested in anything that was sick—human or not. In early childhood she put a splint on a dog's broken leg and nursed a chicken back to health after it had swallowed a fishing hook. At age thirty-two, however, Sanders thought that such a career move, especially for a black woman, would be impossible. Still, her sisters insisted that with their financial help and her job with the National Youth Administration, Maude would be able to finance a medical education.

Because she had no bachelor's degree, Sanders spent two years at Xavier and New Orleans University taking the science courses required for acceptance at the Meharry Medical School in Nashville. However, neither school would accept the courses she had taken at the other and

award her a bachelor's degree. Fortunately, the Meharry Medical School admitted her without the bachelor's degree because she had all of the required science courses.

Maude Sanders and three other women were the first women admitted to Meharry in 1934; one of them (Doris Sanders) graduated with Maude Sanders in 1939. During her years of medical school, Maude Sanders was the oldest student at Meharry and it embarrassed her. Meharry required all women to study for five years—and the men four—in order to graduate.

After graduating from medical school, Sanders faced another hurdle: internship. Most programs discriminated against women and black students, and Sanders was both. She and Doris Sanders were the first women to be accepted at City Hospital (Homer Philips) in St. Louis, Missouri. Denied an opportunity to specialize in surgery, however, Sanders accepted a place in urology. The female interns shared men's quarters and were paid $75 a month, while the men were paid $125 per month. Sanders and the other woman were so happy to have a place to intern that they did not complain.

When Sanders completed her internship, she learned through a friend that the one black male physician in Peoria was leaving. So, in 1942, she relocated. In Peoria she rented quarters that had been vacated by the physician for $25 a month. As the only black physician in Peoria, Sanders' office was always overflowing with patients. Most of her patients were black residents who were too poor to pay, but Sanders served them anyway. Not surprisingly, therefore, Sanders worked from early morning to late at night, and even after she returned home, patients would call and come to her for help. As a general practitioner, she also took on the roles of sister, mother, lawyer, and marriage counselor to her patients.

When Sanders retired in 1990, Mayor James Maloof declared October 17 of that year Maude Sanders Day. Sanders received several other awards for her service to the citizens of Peoria, among them the Martin Luther King, Jr. Award, the United Way Award, the Illinois State Medical Society Award, the Outstanding Business/ Woman Award, the Distinguished Service Award, the Career Center Award, and the Outstanding Physician Award.

As a black female, Sanders had to overcome a great deal of race and sex discrimination, but she never allowed adversity to overcome her principles. For instance, although she was accepted as a member of the Peoria American Medical Society, because the society met at the segregated Jefferson Hotel, she was not allowed to attend meetings. Because of this rebuff, Sanders never attended meetings, even after the policy was changed. Also, a physician once asked Sanders to marry him, but she had to refuse his offer because he did not want her to continue to practice medicine. Relating the incident in an interview, Sanders said, "He didn't want a woman whom he felt might be equal or above his professional ability."

In addition, although Sanders was permitted to practice medicine in three local hospitals, the hospitals themselves were segregated when she came in 1942, and she had problems getting her patients admitted because only a designated number of rooms was allocated for black patients. "We re-sented it," Sanders said. "We fought it for years. They were reluctant to put whites next to blacks. I had patients die before they could get in."

Maud Sanders died in October of 1995.

MILDRED PRATT

Staupers, Mabel Keaton (1890–1989)

The history of black nursing is characterized by a relentless struggle for equality of opportunities, and a quest for recognition and acceptance into the mainstream of American nursing. Although others also played major roles in the advance of black nursing, Mabel Keaton Staupers deserves special recognition. Staupers orchestrated the long struggle of black nurses to win full integration into the American nursing profession during the decades of the Great Depression and World War II. Staupers is perhaps best known for her role in implementing the desegregation of the U.S. Army Nurse Corps during World War II. She published an illuminating account of this and other battles of black nurses in *No Time for Prejudice: A Story of the Integration of Negroes in Nursing in the United States* (1961).

Staupers was born in Barbados, in the West Indies, on February 27, 1890, to Thomas and Pauline Doyle. In April 1903, she and her parents migrated to the United States, settling into the Harlem community in New York City. She completed primary and secondary school there, and in 1914, enrolled in the Freedmen's Hospital School of Nursing (now the **Howard University** College of Nursing) in Washington, D.C. Three years later, she graduated with hon-

Best known for her role in implementing the desegregation of the U.S. Army Nurse Corps during World War II, Mabel Staupers (shown here, center) was a tireless organizer and leader who was one of the founders of the National Council of Negro Women. For her achievements in integrating black nurses into the mainstream, she received the Spingarn Medal in 1951. (MOORLAND-SPINGARN)

ors from the nursing program and was married to Dr. James Max Keaton of Asheville, North Carolina. The marriage, however, ended in divorce. In 1931, she married Fritz C. Staupers of New York City. They remained married until his death in 1949.

When Staupers entered nursing, the vast majority of hospital nurses' training schools denied admission to black women. These exclusionary practices reflected the dominant social system of racial segregation and discrimination in America. In response, African-American leaders embraced the ideology of racial solidarity and black self-help, creating a parallel infrastructure of hospitals and nursing training schools, and founding separate professional societies and organizations.

Like the vast majority of all graduate nurses, Staupers began her professional career by accepting private-duty cases. Opportunities for black women to secure positions in hospital staff nursing and visiting and settlement house or public health nursing were virtually nonexistent. Staupers was an exception in that her career as a private-duty nurse was brief. In 1920, in cooperation with black physicians Louis T. Wright and James Wilson, Staupers helped to organize the Booker T. Washington Sanitarium, the first in-patient center in Harlem for black patients with tuberculosis and one of the few city facilities that permitted black physicians to treat their patients.

Staupers' work with black health care facilities and organizations enlarged her awareness of the discrimination and segregation that African Americans encountered in their search for adequate medical treatment. After she received a 1921 working fellowship at the Henry Phipps Institute of Tuberculosis in Philadelphia, she accepted an assignment at the Jefferson Hospital Medical College. Her firsthand observations of the ill treatment and lack of respect for African Americans by college administrators and physicians left an indelible impression on the young nurse.

In 1922, she accepted an invitation by the New York Tuberculosis and Health Association to conduct a survey of the health needs of residents in the Harlem community. Her subsequent report which found the city's efforts to meet their needs to be inadequate, led to the establishment of the Harlem Committee of the New York Tuberculosis and Health Association. For twelve years, Staupers served as the organization's executive secretary. She worked assiduously to channel aid and resources to members of minority groups afflicted with tuberculosis.

In 1934, Staupers became executive secretary of the **National Association of Colored Graduate Nurses** (NACGN) just as **Estelle Massey Osborne** (1903–1981), the superintendent of nurses at the Homer G. Phillips Hospital in St. Louis, Missouri, assumed the presidency. In 1931, Osborne had become the first black nurse to earn a master of arts degree in nursing education. Together, Staupers and Osborne worked to win acceptance and integration of black nurses into the mainstream of American nursing. Both women also joined **Mary McLeod Bethune** in 1935 in founding the **National Council of Negro Women.**

The NACGN's fight for nursing integration involved a series of strategies, the first of which was to institute programs that addressed the immediate needs of black nurses. Staupers spent the first few years in her new position collecting data, organizing state and local nursing associations, advising and counseling black nurses, and representing them in the larger community. She organized a biracial national advisory council in 1938 in order to develop greater public interest in and support for the association's programs among prominent liberal white groups.

The struggle acquired new momentum and urgency with the outbreak of World War II. Staupers adroitly seized the opportunity created by the war emergency and the increased demand for nurses to project the plight of black nurses into the national limelight. By the time of the Japanese attack on Pearl Harbor in December 1941, Staupers had honed her sharp sense of political timing. When the army set a quota of fifty-six black nurses and the navy refused even to consider admitting black nurses into the Army Nurse Corps, Staupers swung the NACGN into action.

She publicized the denial of opportunities to black nurses who desired to serve their country and joined with other black leaders in meeting directly with army generals and high-ranking government officials to protest the imposition of quotas. Although the pressure resulted in little immediate success, shortly before the war ended, black nurses were able to claim victory in their battle against discriminatory quotas and second-class treatment in the military and the civilian nursing professions.

Exhausted by the battle to integrate blacks into the Army and Navy Nurse Corps, she relinquished her position as executive secretary of the NACGN in 1946 to take a much-needed rest. It was to be of short duration, however, since Staupers had not yet accomplished her major objective: the integration of black women into the American Nurses Association (ANA). Since 1934, Staupers and Osborne had been pressuring the ANA to integrate at its biennial meetings. In 1948, the ANA opened its doors to black membership.

Staupers was elected president of the NACGN in 1949. With the removal of the overtly discriminatory barriers to membership in the ANA, Staupers and the leadership of the NACGN persuaded its members that the organization was now obsolete. The ANA agreed to take over the functions of the NACGN and to continue to award the **Mary Mahoney** Medal to the individual or group contributing the most to intergroup relations within a given period. During the NACGN's 1949 convention, the members voted the organization out of existence.

Staupers received many accolades for her leadership. The crowning acknowledgment of her role in, and contribution to the quest of black nurses to gain their civil rights came when the Spingarn Committee of the **National Association for the Advancement of Colored People** chose her to receive the Spingarn Medal for 1951. In 1967, New York mayor John V. Lindsay gave her a citation of appreciation, which read: "To an immigrant who came to the United States and by Individual Effort through Education and Personal Achievement has become an Outstanding American Leader and Distinguished Citizen of America." Three years later, Howard University gave her the Alumni Award "for Distinguished Achievement in the Fields of Nursing and Community Service." Staupers lived with her sister in Washington, D.C., until her death on September 29, 1989.

DARLENE CLARK HINE

Steward, Susan McKinney (1847–1918)

Her patients affectionately referred to her as "Dr. Susan," because this modest but strong-willed physician acted out of a compassionate desire to serve humanity. She was born of mixed European, African, and Shinnecock Indian ancestry in 1847, the seventh of ten children of Sylvanus and Ann S. Smith. Both Sylvanus and his wife Ann Smith were active in civic affairs and members of the Brooklyn black elite. As a child, Susan studied the organ under the tutelage of John Zundel and Henry Eyre Brown, and this musical training made her a welcome addition as organist and chorister at Brooklyn's Siloam Presbyterian

Church and the Bridge Street African Methodist Episcopal (AME) Church.

Susan McKinney Steward entered the New York Medical College for Women in 1867, graduating three years later as class valedictorian. She was the first black female to practice medicine in New York State, and the third in the nation. Her predecessors, **Rebecca Lee [Crumpler]**, a graduate of the New England Female Medical College (1864), and **Rebecca J. Cole,** a graduate of the Woman's Medical College in Philadelphia (1867), never equaled her in social or medical prominence.

There are several possible explanations for Steward's career choice. She may have been shocked by the untimely deaths of two brothers during the Civil War. Also, in 1866, Brooklyn's death rate soared, because of a cholera epidemic. Perhaps Steward's attention to a sick niece convinced her that she could serve as a medical practitioner. In any event, her decision to seek a medical degree in an era when "ladies" either remained at home or sought teaching positions was indicative of her pride and her unwillingness to place limitations on her possibilities.

In the mid-nineteenth century, male editors, physicians, and laymen viewed medicine as being strictly a male domain. Indeed, women physicians were considered to be "unsexed." Fortunately for Steward, homeopathic medical schools welcomed the presence of women.

The New York Medical College for Women, which opened on November 1, 1863, was a homeopathic medical school founded by Clarence Sophia Lozier, a wealthy abolitionist. Lozier was Steward's mentor and close friend until Lozier's death in 1888, and she took special pleasure in seeing her prized student selected by the faculty and fellow students to be valedictorian of the class of 1870. Steward achieved this honor by studying while her classmates

Shocked by the deaths of her two brothers during the Civil War and by Brooklyn's high death rates in 1866 from a cholera epidemic, Susan McKinney Steward entered medical school and became the first black woman to practice medicine in New York State, and only the third black woman physician in the entire United States. (SCHOMBURG CENTER)

slept, for neither fatigue nor the taunts of male medical students during shared clinic hours at Bellevue Hospital could deter her from her goal. Despite her achievement, New York–area newspapers chose not to print her valedictory. The *Courier* did write about the event, but the reporter focused only on her hair and her choice of clothing, going so far as to express the hope that her "modest attire" was a "good sign of the improvement of the African race."

Steward's medical practice was slow in starting, but it began to catch fire as word spread about her skill. As her caseload grew, it also became diverse; Steward's patients were young and old as well as white and black. The *New York Sun,* in an 1887 feature on wealthy black New Yorkers, described her as someone who had "a handsome bank account and lives well." In 1895, the *New York Times* described her Brooklyn address at 205 DeKalb Avenue as being "in the midst of the fashionable quarter of the hill."

Steward was active in the Kings County Homeopathic Medical Society and the Homeopathic Medical Society of the State of New York. It was before the latter society that she presented two important medical papers. The first, presented in 1883, described the case of a pregnant woman who died after contamination by a solution of carbolic acid. The second paper, "Marasmus Infantum," was delivered in 1886.

Childhood diseases were a specialty of Steward, and she reported that marasmus, or a wasting away of the body, was caused by chronic vomiting, diarrhea, worms, and inherited syphilis. She believed that recovery was facilitated by homeopathic treatment.

Despite maintaining a full medical practice and making surgical rounds at the Brooklyn Woman's Homeopathic Hospital and Dispensary, as well as keeping up an affiliation with the Brooklyn Home for Aged Colored People as its attending physician, Steward found time to be a community activist. She was active in the missionary work of the Bridge Street AME Church; she was a devout supporter of female suffrage; and, as president of the Women's Christian Temperance Union Number 6 in Brooklyn, she spoke out about the dangers of alcohol. In 1884, for example, she urged readers of the New York *Freeman* to "graciously" refrain from serving alcoholic beverages during the Christmas holiday season.

Susan McKinney Steward was married twice. She married William G. McKinney, an itinerant preacher, on July 12, 1871. They had two children: William S. McKinney, who was a clergyman in the Protestant Episcopal Church in New York City, and Anna M. Carty, the former wife of M. Louis Holly and a New York City schoolteacher.

William G. McKinney died in 1892. On November 26, 1896, she married Theophilus Gould Steward, chaplain of the Twenty-fifth U.S. Colored Infantry. Steward was a prolific writer of both sacred and secular materials, and Susan accompanied her husband to Montana and other western states until his retirement in 1907. Later, the couple joined the faculty of Wilberforce University in Ohio. The Stewards traveled to Europe for pleasure in 1909, and again in 1911 so that Steward could deliver a paper, "Colored American Women," before the delegates at the First Universal Race Congress in London. In 1914, she presented a paper, "Women in

Medicine," before the National Association of Colored Women's Clubs in Wilberforce, Ohio.

When Susan Steward died on March 7, 1918, W. E. B. DuBois delivered the eulogy. She is buried in Brooklyn's Greenwood Cemetery. Through the persistence of William S. McKinney, Jr., Steward's grandson, the board of education renamed Brooklyn's Junior High School 265 the Dr. Susan Smith McKinney Junior High School in 1974. Black female doctors in the New York/New Jersey/Connecticut area have also honored her memory by naming their medical society after her.

WILLIAM SERAILE

Temple, Ruth Janetta (1892–1984)

Ruth Janetta Temple was born in Natchez, Mississippi, in 1892. Following her father's death, the family moved in 1904 to Los Angeles. Throughout high school, Ruth cared for her five siblings while her mother worked as a practical nurse to support the family. When Ruth's brother was injured in a gunpowder explosion, she became determined to enter the medical field. "At that time I thought that women were nurses. I didn't know they were doctors. When I learned that women were doctors, I said, 'Ah, that's what I want to be.' "

Temple's medical training at Loma Linda University was financed by prominent black activist T. W. Troy and his colleagues. Upon receiving her medical degree in 1918, Temple opened the first health clinic to be located in southeast Los Angeles, an area populated by 250,000 people. Unable to garner the financial support of area institutions so as to subsidize the Los Angeles clinic, Temple and her husband, real estate developer Otis Banks, bought a five-room bungalow in east Los Angeles and converted it into the facility that became the Temple Health Institute. Temple and Banks, displaced by the instruments and furnishings of the Health Institute, slept in a chicken coop behind the clinic.

Temple later instigated the Health Study Club program, which brought together parents, teachers, and schoolchildren to educate the public on health resources available at Temple's own clinic and elsewhere, as well as on general health issues such as nutrition, sex education, immunization, and substance abuse. According to Temple, she developed the first health study club after having helplessly watched a mother in a damp tenement allow her baby to die of pneumonia out of fear of sending him to the hospital or of allowing Temple to treat him with hydrotherapy in his own home. Membership in the program grew to encompass such disparate groups as teenaged street gangs and nightclub owners and patrons. The program itself ultimately expanded beyond the borders of the state.

Temple's internship with the Los Angeles City Maternity Service (1923–28) inspired her to specialize in obstetrics and gynecology. In 1941, the city health department offered her a scholarship to pursue her master's degree at the Yale University School of Public Health. Temple held several key posts in the Los Angeles Public Health Department from 1942 to 1962 and received many awards and presidential accolades for her work in community health. She died in Los Angeles in 1984 at the age of ninety-one.

In 1978, Temple summed up her views on community health responsibility: "I think that people who can give themselves health care should do it. . . . And then I think that where persons cannot, with their best efforts, do the things they need to have done, I think it should be done for them, beautifully, graciously, and without giving them a feeling of accepting charity."

SUSAN SHIFRIN

Thoms, Adah (c. 1870–1943)

Adah Belle Samuels Thoms devoted her life to nursing—working to improve nurse training, to organize and develop the **National Association of Colored Graduate Nurses,** and to provide equal employment opportunities in the American Red Cross and the U.S. Army Nurse Corps. Thoms also documented the struggles of black nurses in *Pathfinders: A History of the Progress of Colored Graduate Nurses* (1929).

Adah Belle Samuels Thoms was born on January 12, c. 1870, in Richmond, Virginia, to Harry and Melvina Samuels. In 1893, she moved to New York City to study elocution and public speaking at the Cooper Union. It did not take her long to realize the need for more remunerative work. After a job at the Woman's Infirmary and School of Therapeutic Massage in New York, Thoms, the only black student in a nursing class of thirty, graduated in 1900.

Upon receipt of her diploma, Thoms worked as a private-duty nurse in New York City and as a staff nurse at St. Agnes Hospital in Raleigh, North Carolina. After only one year as head nurse of St. Agnes, Thoms returned to New York to seek additional training.

The timing of her return to New York was fortuitous. In 1903, Thoms entered the newly organized school of nursing at Lincoln Hospital and Home. Founded in 1893 by a group of white women who despaired over the impoverished plight of black people in the city, Lincoln soon became a major provider of health care. In 1898, the women managers of Lincoln Hospital opened a nursing school for black women. This nursing school soon became one of the most outstanding of the approximately ten black schools of nursing formed during the 1890s. Black communities across the country joined in a nationwide movement to establish a racially separate network of parallel institutions. The entrenchment of racial segregation dictated these actions. By the 1930s, over two hundred black hospitals, with one third of them operating nursing training schools, existed.

Thoms was obviously a talented student nurse. While in her second year at Lincoln, she won appointment to the position of head nurse on a surgical ward, and upon her graduation in 1905, Lincoln immediately offered her full-time employment.

In 1906, Thoms assumed the position of assistant superintendent of nurses, a position she held until her retirement eighteen years later. Only unrelenting racial discrimination can explain the refusal of the white managers to promote Thoms to the superintendency of Lincoln Hospital. Still, as assistant superintendent, Thoms made noteworthy strides in improving nursing training. In 1913, she began a six-month postgraduate course for registered nurses, and in 1917, just five years after the establishment of the National Organization for Public Health Nursing, she inaugurated a course in public health nursing.

As a long-time president of the Lincoln Nurses' Alumnae, Thoms was well situated to respond to a letter from a black nurse, **Martha Franklin.** Thoms informed Franklin of the Lincoln Alumnae Association's willingness to sponsor the first meeting of what would become the National Association of Colored Graduate Nurses (NACGN). While Franklin became president of the new organization, Thoms was elected treasurer. Like many black nurses, Thoms was eager to become more engaged in the profession. The denial of membership in the American Nurses Association (ANA) increased her determination to raise the status of black nurses. Through her association with Franklin, Thoms embraced the prospect of founding a black professional nurses association.

Eventually, Thoms served as president of the NACGN from 1916 to 1923. She fought to improve the training offered in the black hospital nursing schools and became a staunch advocate for providing greater employment opportunities for black nurses. Throughout this period, Thoms set the model for black nurse involvement in a variety of community organizations and concerns. In 1916, she began to work with both the National Urban League and the **National Association for the Advancement of Colored People** in an attempt to improve conditions at black hospitals and training schools. At the top of her agenda was the necessity to build NACGN's membership and to organize local and state associations of black graduate nurses across the country. Of course, little advance was possible on this front until the NACGN found resources sufficient to employ a full-time executive director.

America's entry into World War I signaled a growing need for nurses. Thoms wanted desperately for black nurses to become a part of the war effort. She appreciated the fact that nursing status usually increased during wartime. When Congress declared war on Germany in April 1917,

Thoms urged black nurses to enroll in the American Red Cross Nursing Service, the only avenue into the U.S. Army Nurse Corps. But when black nurses applied to the American Red Cross, they were met by cold, silent rejection.

Thoms engaged in a futile campaign to reverse the Red Cross' refusal to accept black nurses. In the eleventh hour, Jane A. Delano, chair of the American National Red Cross Nursing Service, indicated that she was willing to accept black nurses at home and abroad, but the surgeon general of the army remained adamant. Finally, in December 1917, Thoms received word that there would be limited enrollment of black nurses. Although the first black nurse enrolled in July 1918, it was not until December 1918, after the war was over, that eighteen qualified black nurses were appointed to the Army Nurse Corps with full rank and pay.

Although Thoms did not achieve the objective of having black women participate in the war effort, she did win other kinds of recognition for herself and for black nurses in general. In 1917, she helped to establish a new order of black war nurses, called the Blue Circle Nurses. The Circle for Negro War Relief recruited these nurses and paid them to work in local communities, instructing poor rural black people on the importance of sanitation, proper diet, and appropriate clothing. In 1921, Thoms was appointed by the assistant surgeon general of the army to serve on the Woman's Advisory Council of Venereal Diseases of the United States Public Health Service.

Thoms retired from Lincoln in 1923 and married Henry Smith. The marriage was cut short by his death the following year. After her retirement, she continued to be active in a variety of professional organizations. In 1929, she wrote the first history of black nurses. And in 1936, the NACGN awarded Thoms its first **Mary Mahoney** Award. Thoms died on February 21, 1943. In 1976, Thoms posthumously was named into nursing's Hall of Fame.

DARLENE CLARK HINE

W

Washington, Georgia (1864–1900)

Georgia Patton was the first black woman in Tennessee to be licensed to practice medicine for surgery. Born in Grundy County, Tennessee, in 1864, she graduated from Central Tennessee College in Nashville in 1890 and in 1893, was the first woman to receive a medical degree from Meharry Medical College.

On May 5, 1893, Patton sailed for Liberia as a self-supporting medical missionary. In 1894, she wrote:

> For the first few days after my arrival, the surroundings looked very discouraging for my professional work. On examining my first case, remarks made by natives were "Patients in his condition never get well; we always expect them to die. You may as well give him up; he will die." After careful treatment and watching for two months he was able to leave his bed, and finally went to his work. The next two cases were also considered to be hopeless, yet both recovered.

Patton stated that she lost only four patients out of more than one hundred.

Due to ill health and poor finances, Patton was forced to return to Memphis, where she established a private practice. She married David W. Washington on December 29, 1897, and died only three years later, on November 8, 1900.

JANET MILLER

Wethers, Doris L. (1927–)

Doris L. Wethers is a pediatrician renowned for her part in the fight against sickle-cell anemia. Whether engaging in research, training doctors, or pressing for the use of early screening techniques, Wethers has been in the forefront of the effort.

Born on December 14, 1927, in Passaic, New Jersey, not far from New York City, Wethers is the daughter of William Wethers and Vivian Wilkerson Wethers. Her father was a physician and a graduate of **Howard University** Medical School. He practiced medicine in Passaic until he was called to active service in World War II, where he achieved the rank of major. After the war he moved the family to New York City. He was a founding doctor of the Health Insurance Plan (HIP) Upper Manhattan Group in Harlem.

Doris Wethers attended public schools, graduating with a bachelor of science degree from Queens College in 1948, magna cum laude. She attended Yale University School of Medicine, earning her M.D. in 1952.

After completing her internship and residencies, Wethers spent the next ten years in private practice in an office next to her father's. During this period she deepened her interest in childhood sickle-cell anemia, as well as other children's health issues.

In 1958, Wethers became an assistant in the pediatrics clinic at Saint Luke's Hospital, its first black attending physician. From 1961 to 1973, she was medical director for Speedwell Services for Children, a foster care and adoption agency; from 1965 to 1973, she was also director of pediatrics at Knickerbocker Hospital.

It was at Knickerbocker (later known as the Arthur B. Logan Memorial Hospital) that she began the fight to which she would devote her life. There, she opened a program serving the needs of sickle-cell anemia patients. Sickle-cell anemia is a disease that strikes many young African Americans. For a very long time, little attention was paid to testing black children for the sickle cell or to providing treatment. But Doris Wethers, with her strong commitment to children and to medicine, became a leader in the struggle to defeat this difficult disease.

In 1969, Wethers became director of pediatrics at Sydenham Hospital in New York, remaining there until 1974. While at Sydenham she opened another sickle-cell treatment center, similar to the one at Knickerbocker. In the mid-seventies, both of these hospitals closed. At this point, Wethers became director of pediatrics at Saint Luke's Hospital, where she had worked for many years, and remained in that job until 1979, when Saint Luke's merged with Roosevelt Hospital. To this day, Wethers continues to head the sickle-cell program at the merged hospital. In 1983, Wethers also became director of pediatrics at Manhattan HIP, the organization that her father helped to found. She retired from this position in 1992, although she has continued her work in the sickle-cell anemia program.

Aside from her busy schedule as an attending pediatrician and program director, Wethers has done groundbreaking research. In 1979, she received a grant to study sickle-cell anemia in children and adolescents. Her work focused on the way the disease affects growth and development, and on such complications of the disease as bone and blood infections.

Wethers has long advocated early screening for sickle-cell anemia, including the screening of newborn infants. She also trains medical students in her specialty. St. Luke's/Roosevelt Hospital is now an affiliate of the Columbia School of Medicine. Wethers conducts in-patient rounds with medical students, exposing a new generation of doctors to her lifetime of insights into sickle-cell anemia.

Nothing can be done to prevent sickle-cell anemia, and there remains a great deal to be learned in the management of the disease. For instance, Wethers notes that some cures have been reported from bone-marrow transplants. The disadvantage is that the transplants themselves have a 30 percent mortality rate. Sickle-cell anemia, while painful, is far less fatal than this. While the search for a cure goes on, much can be done to manage some of the disease's more serious complications.

Wethers has contributed more than fifty articles on sickle-cell anemia to various medical and research journals, and she has written books on the care and treatment of the disease for both doctors and non-medical personnel.

Wethers has received numerous honors, including the Southern Christian Leadership Conference Award for Sickle-Cell Anemia in 1972, an Award of Merit from the Public Health Association of New York in 1974, the Charles Drew Memorial Award from Columbia University College of Physicians and Surgeons in 1984, and also in

1984, a recognition award by the Heart-beats of Jamaica, Inc., for her work with children.

Wethers remains active as an attending pediatrician, teaching and exploring treatments for sickle-cell anemia.

ANDRA MEDEA

Whipper, Ionia Rollin   (c. 1874–1953)

Ionia Rollin Whipper, M.D., was born in South Carolina. Her grandfather, William Whipper, was a conductor on the Underground Railroad. A woman's rights activist from Philadelphia, Whipper's father moved to South Carolina, became a circuit court judge, and, in 1868, founded Whipper, Elliott, and Allen, the first black law firm in the United States. He married Frances Rollin, author of *The Life and Public Services of Martin Delaney,* which she published under the pseudonym Frank A. Rollin. In the 1880s, Ionia moved to Washington, D.C., with her mother and there studied medicine at **Howard University** Medical School.

Whipper graduated from Howard in 1903 with a specialty in obstetrics. She practiced in the maternity ward of the Freedmen's Hospital; served as resident physician at the Collegiate Institute in West Virginia; and during the 1920s taught obstetrics, hygiene, and pediatrics at the John A. Andrew Memorial Hospital at the Tuskegee Institute. While at Tuskegee, she also served as assistant and acting medical director and as a physician for women students.

During World War I, under the sponsorship of the War Work Council, Whipper traveled throughout the South, lecturing on health and social hygiene. From 1918 to 1920, she continued this work under the auspices of the national **Young Women's Christian Association** (YWCA). From 1924 through 1929, she again traveled in the Southern states, this time training midwives, recording births, and conducting child health conferences for the Children's Bureau of the U.S. Department of Labor in connection with the 1921 Sheppard-Towner Act, whose purpose was to study and combat infant and maternal mortality.

When her work at the Children's Bureau ended in 1930, Whipper focused her attention on the plight of young unwed mothers in Washington, D.C. Her home became a haven for single mothers in need of shelter and medical care during and after their pregnancies. In the 1930s, she opened a permanent facility on East Capitol Street. For many years, the Ionia R. Whipper Home for Unwed Mothers, now the Dr. Ionia R. Whipper Residence, remained the city's only facility providing shelter and health care for single black mothers.

Whipper died in Washington, D.C., in 1953.

TERESA R. TAYLOR

Woodby-McKane, Alice   (c. 1863–1946)

Dr. Alice Woodby-McKane and her husband, Dr. Cornelius McKane, established the first hospital in Monrovia, Liberia, in 1895.

A Pennsylvania native, Alice Woodby attended Hampton Institute from 1884 until 1886, when she entered the Institute for Colored Youth. After graduation in 1889, she entered the Woman's Medical College of Pennsylvania in 1890 and received her degree in 1892. Soon thereafter she moved to Augusta, Georgia, to establish a practice and to teach at the **Haines Institute.** She married Cornelius McKane, M.D., and they relocated to Savannah, Georgia, where she established the first training school for black nurses in southeast Georgia in 1893.

In 1894, she and her husband went to Monrovia, Liberia, where they established a hospital. Woodby-McKane was also with the Monrovia Poor Home and was an assistant pension examiner for Civil War veterans. In 1896, she returned with her husband to Savannah and established the McKane Hospital for Women and Children.

About 1900, she moved to Boston with her husband and family. In addition to her practice, Woodby-McKane was a lecturer and instructor for nurses at Plymouth Hospital and was active in Massachusetts politics, serving as an elected delegate to the Republican state convention as a precinct leader. She also was director of the South End Cooperative Bank of Boston. She died of arteriosclerosis in Boston on March 6, 1946.

Of her philosophy Woodby-McKane wrote: "I work very hard that I might be able to carry out the Hampton idea of passing along what one has received."

JANET MILLER

Wright, Jane Cooke (1919–)

Cancer researcher, physician, and the first black woman to be the associate dean of a major American medical school, Dr. Jane C. Wright has left her mark on science.

Wright was born on November 30, 1919, in New York City, to Louis T. Wright and Corrine Cooke Wright. Her family had a strong medical tradition. Her father was one of the first black graduates of Harvard University and a prominent surgeon and cancer researcher. At his twenty-fifth Harvard reunion, he was voted the classmate who had contributed most to medical knowledge. Wright's paternal grandfather was among the first graduates of Meharry Medical College. Her step-grandfather was the first African American to earn an M.D. from Yale Medical School. Wright's sister Barbara also became a physician.

Wright was raised in the family home in Harlem. She attended private schools, graduating from high school in 1938. She was awarded a four-year scholarship to Smith College, where she excelled both in academics and on the swim team. She considered a career in art, but as the country was still recovering from the Great Depression, she settled upon a safer career in medicine. Wright graduated from Smith in 1942, then won a four-year scholarship to New York Medical College.

World War II was then in progress. To meet the urgent need for doctors, the normal four-year medical course was compressed into three years of year-round classes. Wright excelled in medical school even with its accelerated program, finding time to be vice president of her class and president of the honor society. She earned an M.D. with honors in 1945, graduating third in a class of ninety-five.

Wright served her internship at Bellevue Hospital from 1945 to 1946. She did her assistant residency the following year at the same hospital. Her final step was her residency in internal medicine, which was done in 1947, at Harlem Hospital.

Now a full physician, Wright took a job as a New York City school physician in 1948, at the same time becoming a visiting physician at Harlem Hospital. That same year she became a clinician at the Cancer Research Foundation at Harlem Hospital, a program that had been founded by her father. Her father died a few years later, in 1952. At that time, she succeeded him as director of the foundation.

The Cancer Research Foundation at Harlem Hospital studied the use of drugs to combat cancer and other tumors. In 1955, Wright was asked to join the faculty of the New York University Medical Center. Her role was director of cancer chemotherapy research and instructor of research surgery within the department of surgery. She soon was promoted to assistant professor. In 1961, she became adjunct professor of research surgery.

In 1967, Wright returned to her alma mater, New York Medical College, as associate dean and professor of surgery. Her duties were to pursue her research and develop a program to study cancer, heart disease, and stroke. These were the three major fatal diseases of the nation. In 1964, she was appointed to the President's Commission on Heart Disease, Cancer, and Stroke. The analysis of the commission led to the establishment of a national network of centers specializing in these diseases.

Aside from these duties, Wright served as vice president of the African Research Foundation. In 1961, she want to East Africa on a medical inspection tour. She also served as personal physician to Mrs. Kwame Nkrumah.

Wright has written more than seventy-five scientific papers on cancer research and received honorary degrees from Women's Medical College (now named Medical College of Pennsylvania) and Denison University. She has served on more than twenty local and national medical committees and received numerous awards for her work in medicine.

Early in her career, she earned a Merit Award for 1952 from *Mademoiselle*. This award was reserved for women in their twenties and early thirties "who have already distinguished themselves in their fields and are expected to achieve even greater honors." In 1965, she received the Spirit of Achievement Award of the Women's Division of the Albert Einstein College of Medicine. The award cited her "deep commitment as a scientist and teacher in advancing medical knowledge and research." In 1967, she received the Hadassah Myrtle Wreath award for outstanding contribution to her field of endeavor. This was an honor shared with some of the most famous humanitarians of her time, including noted writer Elie Wiesel.

An emeritus professor since 1987, Wright is now semi-retired. A brilliant woman who maintained a long and remarkable career, she served the cause of science in its battle against one of the most feared diseases of our era. She also furthered the cause of women in medicine. "I want to see a time in this country," she has said, "when a woman in medicine is not such an outstanding exception. I want to see a time when everyone with a bent for medicine is in the field, contributing to better health care for all of us. I want to see a time when people with special talent, whatever their sex, take their place in making the world free of disease."

ANDRA MEDEA

Y

Young, Jean Wheeler (1942–)

The 1960s were life-changing times, particularly for those involved in the civil rights movement. For Detroit native Jean Wheeler Smith Young (who was born on April 9, 1942), a Washington, D.C., psychiatrist, writer, and former civil rights organizer in Mississippi and southwest Georgia, the movement continues to inform and enhance both her personal and professional lives. "My work with the **Student Nonviolent Coordinating Committee** (SNCC) was extremely fulfilling," she has said, "because it involved empowering groups of people and nurturing their ability, as a community, to act in their own behalf. Professionally, these are the same goals I have as a psychiatrist, though I now work on a more individual basis."

The movement also enabled Young to juggle a variety of responsibilities. This proved to be a necessity when she decided, in the late 1960s, to return to college to pursue a master's degree in food science and nutrition, having studied premed and graduated Phi Beta Kappa with a B.S. in chemistry from **Howard University** in 1965. While studying for her master's degree, she raised two children, Malaika and Tarik, with the help of her former husband, D.C. City Council Chair Frank Smith. She also continued to write, receiving acclaim for her many published works, both fiction and nonfiction.

From 1970 to 1975, she was assistant professor in the Department of Interdisciplinary Sciences at the fledgling Federal City College, now the University of the District of Columbia. Never having lost her love of medicine, she decided to enter George Washington University Medical School. She graduated in 1980 and completed her residency in psychiatry, with a fellowship in child and adolescent psychology, at the university's medical center in 1985.

Always the juggler, Young currently is medical director of the women's unit of the Psychiatric Institute of Washington, while also maintaining a private practice targeted to young people and serving as a consultant to several inner-city mental health programs. In this context, she serves as division chief of children's services for the Center for Family Health of the D.C. Institute of Mental Health, where the grant that she cowrote allows her to develop her specialty: the treatment of children traumatized by violence and vulnerable to the lure of drug addiction.

Young continues to bear witness to the movement that helped shape her. As she wrote in a 1966 essay in the *New Republic*: "It's too hard to find ways of giving people decent places to stay and livable incomes. It is hard because we're told that to decide to do this is also to make decisions about national fiscal policy and the social order

131

and labor unions and the international balance of payments. And we cringe before these weighty matters. . . . I think people can get loose from the fear of deciding about things that are important by trying to consider and deal with the problems of people at the bottom."

This philosophy guides Young's practice and her life. She is supported in this by her husband, James Young, a computer program manager and retired chemist.

JUDY RICHARDSON

Young, Roger Arliner (1889–1964)

Few black women in the United States had the opportunity to engage in scientific research in the decades before World War II. Due to educational, racial, and sexual barriers, few black women produced work that would allow them to lay full claim to the title of scientist. Roger Arliner Young, the first black woman to earn a doctoral degree in zoology (University of Pennsylvania, 1940), was also one of the first black women to conduct and publish research in her field. In 1924, working first with her mentor, noted black zoologist Ernest Everett Just, she made a significant contribution to the study of the structures that control salt concentration in paramecium. Later she also published several notable studies on the effects of direct and indirect radiation on sea urchin eggs.

Born in Clifton Forge, Virginia, Young entered **Howard University** in 1916. After graduating in 1923, she was hired there as an assistant professor of zoology. She received a master's degree in zoology in 1926 from the University of Chicago, where she was elected to Sigma Xi. From 1927 until 1936, she spent summers doing research at the leading biological research institution in the country, the Marine Biological Laboratory in Woods Hole, Massachusetts.

Although she was successful at both research and teaching, Young began to experience difficulties in both areas during the 1930s. Burdened by a heavy teaching load and a lack of financial resources, she began to flounder. However, after losing her position at Howard University in 1935, she rallied to continue her research, publishing four papers between 1935 and 1938 and completing her doctoral work at the University of Pennsylvania under L. V. Heilbrunn in 1940. From 1940 to 1947, she taught at the North Carolina College for Negroes and at Shaw University, also in North Carolina. During the 1950s, she taught at several black colleges in Texas, Louisiana, and Mississippi. Unfortunately, by the early 1960s she had succumbed to the effects of continuing personal and professional difficulties. Young died on November 9, 1964.

A successful scientific career is predicated on stable institutional affiliations, manageable teaching loads, financial support for research, and the continuing support of mentors, peers, and community; Young had few of these benefits throughout her career. Scientific achievement, however, is measured largely by the quality of the research produced; by this measure, Young was a success. Further, she displayed one of the most abiding characteristics of all good scientists: a commitment to furthering science against all odds.

EVELYNN M. HAMMONDS

Chronology

1850

Lucy Sessions earns a literary degree from **Oberlin College,** becoming the first black woman in the United States to receive a college degree.

1862

Susie King Taylor, at fourteen, becomes the first African-American army nurse.

1864

Rebecca Lee Crumpler becomes the first African-American woman to graduate from a U.S. college with a formal medical degree, and the first and only black woman to obtain the "Doctress of Medicine" degree from the New England Female Medical College in Boston.

1867

Rebecca Cole, the second black woman to receive a medical degree in the U.S., graduates from the Women's Medical College of Pennsylvania.

1868

The **Howard University** Medical School is chartered and is supported by the U.S. government as an institution to train African Americans.

1869

Howard University Medical School opens its doors to women both black and white; by 1900, 103 women have enrolled; 48 of these women—23 black women and 25 white women—go on to graduate.

1873

The first three American nurse training schools are established. By 1926, there are 2,150 schools, virtually all of which exclude black women.

1879

Mary Eliza Mahoney graduates from the New England Hospital for Women and Children nurses' training program.

1883

Rebecca Lee Crumpler, M.D., publishes *A Book of Medical Discourses in Two Parts.* Based on nearly two decades of practice as a physician, it offers advice to women on how to provide medical care to themselves and their children.

1885

Sara E. Goode is the first black woman to receive a U.S. patent, for her "Folding Cabinet Bed."

1886

John D. Rockefeller contributes the funds for the establishment of a school of nursing at the Atlanta Baptist Seminary (now **Spelman College**), a school for black women. This is the first school of nursing established within an academic institution in the country.

1887

Mary Ellen Morrison earns a pharmaceutical doctor degree from Howard University's School of Medicine.

1888

Verina Morton Jones graduates from the Woman's Medical College of Pennsylvania and becomes the first black woman to practice medicine in Mississippi.

Miriam E. Benjamin is awarded a patent for a "Gong and Signal Chair," which is later adopted for use in the U.S. House of Representatives to signal pages.

1890

Ida Gray becomes the first African-American woman to receive the doctor of dental surgery degree, from the University of Michigan.

1891

Daniel Hale Williams, the famed open-heart surgeon, establishes Provident Hospital and Nurse Training School in Chicago.

Halle Tanner Dillon Johnson graduates from the Woman's Medical College of Pennsylvania and becomes the first black woman to practice medicine in Alabama. She serves as the first black woman resident physician at Tuskegee Institute, from 1891 to 1894.

1892

The Tuskegee Institute School of Nurse Training is founded.

The Hampton Nurse Training School at Dixie Hospital in Hampton, Virginia, begins to accept students.

A patent is awarded to Sarah Boone of New Haven, Connecticut, for an improved ironing board.

Anna Mangin of Woodside, New York, patents an improved pastry fork.

1893

Seventeen years after its opening, Meharry Medical College graduates its first black women physicians, Annie D. Gregg and Georgiana Esther Lee Patton.

Sarah Jones graduates from Howard University Medical School and becomes the first woman to pass the Virginia medical board examinations. She later founds the Richmond Hospital and Training School of Nurses, which in 1902 is renamed the Sarah G. Jones Memorial Hospital.

1894

Lucy Hughes Brown graduates from the Woman's Medical College of Pennsylvania and becomes the first black woman to practice medicine in South Carolina.

The Freedmen's Hospital and Nurse Training School is founded in Washington, D.C.

1895

The National Medical Association is founded.

1896

The black women of the **Phyllis Wheatley Club** found the only black hospital and nurse training school in New Orleans. This institution is later renamed the Flint Goodridge Hospital and Nurse Training School.

1897

Alonzo Clifton McClennan founds the Hospital and Nursing Training School in Charleston, South Carolina. **Anna De Costa Banks,** one of the first graduates of the Dixie Hospital School of Nursing, is the first head nurse of the South Carolina institution.

The American Negro Academy is founded to promote scholarly work and fellowship among leading intellectuals. **Anna Julia Cooper** is the only woman elected to membership.

1898

Matilda Evans, the first black woman to practice in South Carolina, establishes three hospitals between 1898 and 1916.

1900

The Woman's Medical College of Pennsylvania, established in 1850 as the first regular medical school for women, has graduated approximately a dozen black women physicians.

1900 to 1920

Only 9 percent of women physicists are employed outside of women's colleges during this time.

1903

Ionia R. Whipper succeeds Halle Johnson as resident physician at Tuskegee Institute. Because of sexist attitudes toward women, Whipper is restricted to the care of female students at the institute.

1905

The Woman's Improvement Club of Indianapolis, Indiana, opens an outdoor tuberculosis camp, purportedly the first in the nation.

1908

Fifty-two nurses convene at St. Mark's Episcopal Church in New York City to found the **National Association of Colored Graduate Nurses** (NACGN).

1911

The American Nurses Association (ANA) is founded. Most of its local affiliates exclude black women.

1912

Adah B. Thoms is one of three black delegates to the International Council of Nurses in Cologne, Germany.

1914

Black midwives attend approximately half of all births in Virginia.

1915

The Association for the Study of Negro Life and History is founded by Carter G. Woodson. Much of its early support comes from black women.

1916

Frances Elliott Davis is the first African-American nurse to enroll officially in the Red Cross nursing service.

1917

Black women develop the Circle for Negro War Relief to provide, among other things, medical service to black soldiers.

1918

The Women's Political Association of Harlem is one of the first African-American organizations in the country to advocate birth control.

1920

Sixty-five black women are practicing medicine in the United States.

The Universal African Black Cross Nurses, a female auxiliary of the **Universal Negro Improvement Association,** is organized.

There are thirty-six black nurse training schools in the United States.

1921

The first black women to earn Ph.D. degrees in the U.S. are **Georgiana R. Simpson,** University of Chicago; **Sadie Tanner Mossell [Alexander],** University of Pennsylvania; and, **Eva Dykes,** Radcliffe College.

1924

Mary Jane Watkins receives a doctor of dental surgery degree and goes on to become the first woman dentist in the military services.

1925

The Rockefeller Foundation employs Ethel Johns to examine the status of black women in the nursing profession. After visiting twenty-three hospitals and nurse training schools for black women, Johns reports appalling conditions.

1926

May Chinn becomes the first black woman intern at Harlem Hospital.

1928

Carrie E. Bullock founds and edits the NACGN's official publication, the *National News Bulletin.*

1930

Matilda Evans establishes a free mother-and-child clinic in the basement of a black church.

1931

Virginia Alexander establishes the Aspiranto Health Home in 1931 to provide health care for poor women and children in North Philadelphia.

Ionia R. Whipper purchases property and opens the Ionia R. Whipper Home for Unwed Mothers, which has a policy of nondiscrimination as to race, religion, or residence.

1935

Dorothy Ferebee directs the **Alpha Kappa Alpha** Mississippi Health Project, which brings much-needed health care to the poor of the Mississippi Delta every summer from 1935 to 1942.

Jessie Jarue Mark is the first African-American woman to earn a Ph.D. in botany (Iowa State University).

1936

Flemmie P. Kittrell is the first African-American woman to earn a Ph.D. in nutrition (Cornell University).

Sixty-seven percent of all North Carolinian black women giving birth are attended by black midwives.

1939

Tuskegee Institute establishes a school of nurse-midwifery.

1940

Roger Arliner Young is the first African-American woman to earn a Ph.D. in zoology (Western Reserve University).

1941

Ruth Lloyd is the first African-American woman to earn a Ph.D. in astronomy (Western Reserve University).

1942

Margurite Thomas is the first African-American woman to earn a Ph.D. degree in geology (Catholic University).

1943

Mamie Phipps Clark becomes the first black woman to earn a Ph.D. in psychology from Columbia University. Her research into the racial identity formation of black children (with her husband, Kenneth Clark) will become central evidence cited in the 1954 *Brown* v. *Board of Education* Supreme Court decision.

1944

Daisy Hill Northcross founds and becomes superintendent of Mercy Hospital in Detroit, Michigan.

1945

The War Department declares that nurses will be accepted into the Army Nurse Corps and the Navy Nurse Corps without regard to race.

Inventor Henrietta Bradbury, going well beyond the sphere of "women's work," develops a "Torpedo Discharge Means" using compressed air.

1946

Margaret Lawrence becomes the first black trainee at the Columbia Psychoanalytic Clinic.

Helen O. Dickens, the daughter of a former slave, receives her certification from the American Board of Obstetrics and Gynecology. Four years later, she becomes the first black woman to be admitted to the American College of Surgeons.

1947

Marie M. Daly is the first African-American woman to earn a Ph.D. in chemistry (Columbia University).

1948

The ANA opens the gates to black membership, appoints a black nurse as assistant executive secretary in its national headquarters, and elects **Estelle Osborne** to the board of directors.

1949

Flemmie P. Kittrell is a U.S delegate to the International Congress of Home Economics in Stockholm, Sweden.

Marjorie Lee Brown (University of Michigan) and **Evelyn Boyd Granville** (Yale University) are the first African-American women to earn Ph.D. degrees in mathematics.

1950

The majority of childbearing black women in Alabama still rely on the care of granny midwives.

1951

The National Association of Colored Graduate Nurses (NACGN) merges with the American Nurses Association (ANA).

Mildred Fay Johnson is the first African-American woman to graduate from Harvard University's Medical School. She goes on to serve three terms as president of the National Right to Life Committee.

Life magazine features Maude Daniels Callen's work as a midwife in South Carolina.

1956
Mary B. D. Kenner, the most prolific African-American woman inventor to date, patents the first of five inventions she will conceive between 1956 and 1987, devices ranging from health aids to household conveniences.

1958
Edith Irby Jones breaks the racial barriers of Southern medical schools when she becomes the first black person, male or female, to be admitted to the University of Arkansas School of Medicine.

1959
Lena Frances Edwards, M.D., subsidizes the founding of Our Lady of Guadelupe Maternity Clinic in Hereford, Texas, to provide medical services to migrant workers.

1960
The doors of most medical schools in the United States are still closed to all women, black and white.

1964
Lena Frances Edwards, M.D. receives the highest civilian award, the Presidential Medal of Freedom, from President Lyndon Baines Johnson. She is the only obstetrician/gynecologist to be so honored.

1968
Hughenna L. Gauntlett is the first black woman to be certified by the American Board of Surgery.

1970
The number of black women practicing medicine in the United States has increased to 1,051.

Effie O'Neal Ellis, M.D., becomes special assistant for health services to the American Medical Association, and is the first black woman physician to hold an administrative post at the executive level in the AMA.

1971
Lauranne B. Sams is a founding member of the National Black Nurses Association and serves as its first president.

1972
Serving as executive director of the New Jersey Medical School College of Medicine and Dentistry, Florence Gaynor becomes the first woman to head a major teaching hospital.

1973
Vernice Ferguson is the first African-American nurse to become chief, Nursing Department, National Institutes of Health.

1976
Josephine Riley Matthews ("Mama Jo"), credited with delivering more than 1,300 babies in South Carolina, is named that state's Woman of the Year and Outstanding Older American.

Shirley A. Jackson is the first black woman in the United States to earn a doctorate in physics, from the Massachusetts

Institute of Technology (MIT). The first black man to receive a physics doctorate did so in 1876, one hundred years before.

1977

In cutting Medicaid funds for abortions, the Hyde Amendment effectively denies many women the option of abortion.

1978

Faye Wattleton becomes the first black person, and the first woman, to serve as president of the Planned Parenthood Federation of America.

1979

When appointed brigadier general in the U.S. Army Nurse Corps, **Hazel Johnson** becomes the first black woman general in the history of the U.S. military. She is also appointed chief of the Army Nurse Corps, the first African American to hold that position.

Jenny Patrick is the first black woman in the U.S. to earn a Ph.D. in chemical engineering (Massachusetts Institute of Technology).

1980

With *Harris* v. *McRae*, the U.S. Supreme Court upholds the cutoff of Medicaid funds for abortion.

Valerie Thomas receives a patent for her "Illusion Transmitter," a "three-dimensional illusional television-like system." Thomas is a data analyst for the National Aeronautics and Space Administration (NASA).

1980s

Black women have gained parity with black men in the sciences, earning 50 percent of all doctorates awarded to black Americans.

1981

The National Black Women's Health Project is founded under the leadership of **Byllye Y. Avery.**

1982

The first national conference on black women's health issues is sponsored by the National Black Women's Health Project under the direction of Byllye Y. Avery.

1983

Christine Darden is the first black woman in the U.S. to earn a Ph.D. degree in mechanical engineering (George Washington University).

1984

Alexa Canady is the first black woman to be certified by the American Board of Neurological Surgery.

1985

Edith Irby Jones becomes the first woman president of the National Medical Association, a predominantly black medical society.

1987

When **Mae Jemison** joins NASA, she is the first black woman to be accepted as an astronaut.

1989

The number of black women practicing medicine in the United States grows to 3,250, but this represents less than 1 percent of the practicing physicians in the United States.

1990
Roselyn Payne Epps, M.D., becomes the first black woman to serve as president of the American Medical Association (AMA).

1991
Vivian Pinn-Wiggins is appointed the first permanent director of the National Institutes of Health (NIH) Office of Women's Health Research.

1992
On September 12, Mae Jemison becomes the first black woman in space, spending a week on the shuttle *Endeavour.* She took with her an Alvin Ailey American Dance Theater poster depicting the dance *Cry,* explaining to **Judith Jamison,** the director of the company, that the dance was created for Jemison and "all black women everywhere."

1993
Hazel O'Leary becomes secretary of energy.

Joycelyn Elders is named surgeon general of the United States.

Bibliography

GENERAL BOOKS USEFUL TO THE STUDY OF BLACK WOMEN IN AMERICA

Reference Books

African-Americans: Voices of Triumph. Three-volume set: *Perseverance, Leadership,* and *Creative Fire.* By the editors of Time-Life Books, Alexandria, Virginia, 1993.

Estell, Kenneth, ed., *The African-American Almanac.* Detroit, Mich., 1994.

Harley, Sharon. *The Timetables of African-American History: A Chronology of the Most Important People and Events in African-American History.* New York, 1995.

Hine, Darlene Clark. *Hine Sight: Black Women and The Re-Construction of American History.* Brooklyn, New York, 1994.

Hine, Darlene Clark, ed., Elsa Barkley Brown, and Rosalyn Terborg-Penn, associate eds. *Black Women in America: An Historical Encyclopedia.* Brooklyn, New York, 1993.

Hornsby, Alton, Jr. *Chronology of African-American History: Significant Events and People from 1619 to the Present.* Detroit, Michigan, 1991.

Kranz, Rachel. *Biographical Dictionary of Black Americans.* New York, 1992.

Lanker, Brian. *I Dream a World: Portraits of Black Women Who Changed America.* New York, 1989.

Logan, Rayford W., and Michael R. Winston, eds. *Dictionary of American Negro Biography.* New York, 1982.

Low, W. Augustus, and Virgil A. Clift, eds. *Encyclopedia of Black America.* New York, 1981.

Salem, Dorothy C., ed. *African American Women: A Biographical Dictionary.* New York, 1993.

Salzman, Jack, David Lionel Smith, and Cornel West. *Encyclopedia of African-American Culture and History.* Five vols. New York, 1996.

Smith, Jessie Carney, ed., *Notable Black American Women,* two vols. Detroit, Mich., Book I, 1993; Book II, 1996.

General Books about Black Women

Giddings, Paula. *When and Where I Enter: The Impact of Black Women on Race and Sex in America.* New York, 1984.

Guy-Sheftall, Beverly. *Words of Fire: An Anthology of African-American Feminist Thought.* New York, 1995.

Hine, Darlene Clark, Wilma King, and Linda Reed, eds. *"We Specialize in the Wholly Impossible": A Reader in Black Women's History.* Brooklyn, N.Y., 1995.

Jones, Jacqueline. *Labor of Love, Labor of Sorrow: Black Women, Work, and the Family from Slavery to the Present.* New York, 1985.

Lerner, Gerda, ed. *Black Women in White America: A Documentary History.* New York, 1972.

BOOKS ABOUT BLACK WOMEN IN SCIENCE, HEALTH, AND MEDICINE

Carnegie, M. Elizabeth. *The Path We Tread: Blacks in Nursing, 1854–1990.* Second ed. New York, 1991.

Distinguished African American Scientists of the 20th Century. Kidd, Renee, and others. Phoenix, Arizona, 1995.

Hine, Darlene Clark. *Black Women in White: Racial Conflict in the Nursing Profession, 1890–1950.* Bloomington, Indiana, 1989.

Sammons, Vivian Ovelton. *Blacks in Science and Medicine.* New York, 1990.

Contents of the Set

(ORGANIZED BY VOLUME)

Education

Social Activism

Contents of the Set

(LISTED ALPHABETICALLY BY ENTRY)

151

Index

Page numbers in **boldface** indicate main entries. Page numbers in *italics* indicate illustrations.

Occupations Index

Volume Codes

B	Business and Professions	M	Music
D	Dance, Sports & Visual Arts	R	Religion
EA	Early Years	SC	Science & Medicine
ED	Education	SO	Social Activists
LA	Law & Government	T	Theater Arts &
LI	Literature		Entertainment

A

Abolitionists

Craft, Ellen EA:73–74
Douglass, Anna Murray
  EA:78–80
Douglass, Sarah Mapps
  EA:80–81
Forten Sisters EA:89–92
Freeman, Elizabeth
  EA:94–95
Grimké, Charlotte
  EA:100–103
Harper, Frances Ellen
  LI:95–100
Jacobs, Harriet Ann
  EA:111–114, LI:114
Pleasant, Mary Ellen
  B:125–127
Prince, Nancy Gardner
  EA:146–147
Remond, Sarah Parker
  EA:149–150
Rollin Sisters EA:152–154
Ruffin, Josephine St. Pierre
  EA:154–158

Truth, Sojourner
  EA:174–178
Tubman, Harriet
  EA:178–182

Actresses and Entertainers

Alice, Mary T:49–51
Allen, Billie T:51–52
Allen, Debbie T:52–54
Archer, Osceola T:55–57
Avery, Margaret T:57
Bailey, Pearl M:56–58
Baker, Josephine D:16–20
Bassett, Angela T:58–59
Beavers, Louise T:60–62
Belgrave, Cynthia T:62–63
Bentley, Gladys T:63
Berry, Halle T:63–64
Bowman, Laura T:65–68
Bricktop (Ada Smith)
  B:50–51
Burke, Georgia T:68–69
Burrows, Vinnie T:70–71
Bush, Anita T:71–72
Canty, Marietta T:73
Cara, Irene M:86–87
Carroll, Diahann T:73–75

Carroll, Vinnette T:75–76
Carter, Nell T:76–77
Cash, Rosalind T:77–78
Childress, Alice T:78–80
Clough, Inez T:80–81
Cole, Olivia T:81–82
Dandridge, Dorothy
  T:83–86
Dandridge, Ruby T:86
Davis, Henrietta Vinton
  SO:71–73
Dee, Ruby T:88–91
Dickerson, Glenda T:91–92
Douglas, Marion T:92–94
Ellis, Evelyn T:96
Foster, Frances T:99–101
Foster, Gloria T:101–102
Gentry, Minnie T:104–105
Gibbs, Marla T:105–106
Gilbert, Mercedes
  T:106–107
Goldberg, Whoopi
  T:107–109
Grant, Micki T:109–111
Grier, Pamela T:111–112

173

L

Labor Organizers
Law Enforcement Officers
Lawyers and Jurists

Master Index
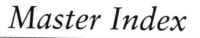

Index

Page numbers in **boldface** indicate main entries. Page numbers in *italics* indicate illustrations.

Volume Codes

B	Business and Professions		M	Music
D	Dance, Sports & Visual Arts		R	Religion
EA	Early Years		SC	Science & Medicine
ED	Education		SO	Social Activists
LA	Law & Government		T	Theater Arts &
LI	Literature			Entertainment

A

Abashing Anomaly, An
  (Sizemore) ED:139
Abbey, Charlotte SC:55
Abbott, Cleveland D:59, 111, 138
Abbott, Jessie D:60, 139
Abbott, Loretta D:12
Abbott, Robert B:54, 63
Abeng (Cliff) LI:53
Abernathy, Ralph SO:67–68
abolitionism LA:9–10; SO:4–6
"Abuse of Liberty, The" (Purvis) EA:90
Ackamoor, Idris SO:109
ACLU *see* American Civil Liberties Union
ACTION
  and Dorothy Cotton SO:68
Adair, Euretta SO:19, 191
Adam of Ife: Black Women in Praise of Black Men (Madgett) LI:130
Adams, Catherine Jackson M:170, 171, *171*, 252

Adams, Howard SC:31
Adams, John EA:162
Adams, Sadie L. SO:30
Adams-Ender, Clara Leach B:28; SC:**33–34**
Addams, Jane SO:139
Adderly, Cannonball M:283
Addison, Adele M:**41**, *41*, 290
Adolescence and Poverty: Challenge for the '90s (Edelman and Ladner) ED:105
Adulthood Rites (Butler) LI:44, 46–47
Adventures of the Dread Sisters (Deveaux) LI:64
AFL *see* American Federation of Labor
AFL-CIO *see* American Federation of Labor–Congress of Industrial Organizations
Aframerican Woman's Journal R:159, 161
Africa Dream (Greenfield) LI:89
Africa: Land of My Fathers (Thompson) B:150

Afric-American Female Intelligence Society, Boston EA:202; SO:195
Africa, My Africa! (Burroughs) LI:43
Africana
  and Ethel Waters T:11
African American Art and Artists (Lewis) D:157
African-American Encyclopedia EA:107
African Americans: Voices of Triumph
  and Rosalyn Andrews B:37–38
African Association for Mutual Relief SO:194
African Blood Brotherhood SO:200
African Colonization Society SO:195
African Dorcas Association EA:148, 201
African Female Benevolent Society, Newport, Rhode Island EA:29, 201